World University Library

The World University Library is an international series
of books, each of which has been specially commissioned.
The authors are leading scientists and scholars from all over
the world who, in an age of increasing specialization, see the
need for a broad, up-to-date presentation of their subject.
The aim is to provide authoritative introductory books for
students which will be of interest also to the general
reader. Publication of the series takes place in Britain,
France, Germany, Holland, Italy, Spain, Sweden and
the United States.

Lucy Mair

Witchcraft

World University Library

McGraw-Hill Book Company
New York Toronto

Library of Congress Catalog Card Number 68–21850
Phototypeset by BAS Printers Limited, Wallop, Hampshire, England
Printed by Officine Grafiche Arnoldo Mondadori, Verona, Italy

Contents

1 Why should there be witches?

In many parts of the world people believe that it is possible for human beings to cause harm to their fellows by the exercise of powers not possessed by ordinary folk, powers which operate in a manner that cannot be detected, so that the cause can only be recognised when the damage comes to light. The persons who are supposed to have these powers are commonly called witches, and the powers, whatever they are supposed to be, are called by a variety of terms. 'Magical' is one that has a respectable ancestry, since it derives from the name of the wise men of the East; but it is nowadays used more often for esoteric means of producing beneficial results. 'Supernatural' would satisfy many of us, but purists argue that those peoples who take the existence of witchcraft for granted regard it, along with good magic, as part of the natural order of things. Some people use the word 'non-empirical' of phenomena the existence of which cannot be tested. Evans-Pritchard, the leading anthropological writer on witchcraft in Africa, the continent where contemporary witchcraft has been most closely studied, prefers 'mystical', and this is the one that I shall use.

Folklorists are interested in the ideas that people have had about the kind of sinister things that witches can do, and psychologists are interested in ideas about the kind of sinister people witches are. Historians, in our enlightened centuries, have tended to concentrate on the absurdity of these beliefs and to ask why they were taken seriously for so long. Contemplating the trials of witches in Europe for acts that are patently impossible, and the tortures by which many were forced to confess to such acts, they have moved from indignation at the injustice to astonishment at the credulity of men, the leading intellectuals of their day, who could compile tracts on demonology as a branch of science.

This book is concerned for the most part with the ideas of witchcraft held today by peoples who have little acquaintance with modern science, and starts from the premise that in a world where

The scene on the lowest rung of this carved chair, made for a Tshokwe chief on the Angola-Congo border, represents a diviner with his bowl, to whom a sick person is being presented for consultation.

there are few assured techniques for dealing with everyday crises, notably sickness, a belief in witches, or the equivalent of one, is not only not foolish, it is indispensable. To this argument one might add that, although some people in the technically sophisticated world really understand the natural sciences, the majority do not; all most of us know is where to go for explanations, particularly in the commonest form of disaster, sickness. We accept the doctor's advice as we might once have accepted that of the diviner who told us whether we were suffering through the anger of an ancestor's spirit or the hatred of a witch. We are more willing perhaps than our ancestors would have been to regard an accident as a matter of chance, though many of us do try to avoid types of action proverbially supposed to be unlucky.

Can we then simply dismiss the belief in witchcraft as a superstition of the ignorant? Certainly ignorance contributes to it. The ordinary unsophisticated member of a technological society may not understand much about germs, but he has heard of them, he knows that, whatever explanation the doctor gives, it will not consist in accusing someone else of causing the illness, and, whatever the prescription, it will not be a recommendation to go and beat up a neighbour until he withdraws his evil influence. Beliefs in witchcraft flourish in societies with inadequate medical knowledge – where there may be a few simple remedies, but for the most part those who fall ill must simply let the illness run its course. Anthropologists sometimes remark that the belief in witchcraft is characteristic of small-scale societies, in which every individual passes his life in the company of a limited number of people personally known to him. If this were taken to mean that there is something in the nature of such societies particularly conducive to the development of a belief in witchcraft, it might be misleading. One might better say that it is the development of scientific techniques – which include medical knowledge – that has brought into being the large-scale societies of the modern world. It is in the absence of such knowledge that people *both* live in small, closely circumscribed communities *and* explain sickness and misfortune by witchcraft.

Nobody is willing to resign himself to a sickness with no remedy. The sick person and his family need to feel that something is being done to help recovery; indeed in Africa it is usually held to be the duty of the head of the family to find out what should be done. This may be a matter of finding simple remedies; and these may or may not be effective. But there must be somewhere a theory of causation which can account for the serious cases; and this is the theory that sickness, along with other misfortunes such as barrenness of women or cattle, destruction of crops by a sudden storm, a bad harvest when your neighbour has a good one, or even some unexplained accident such as falling off a ladder, is sent by personalised beings, either spirits who have authority to punish you or humans who envy or hate you. Death too, although it is irremediable, must be assigned a cause.

A significant part of witch-lore is that which attributes to witches actions that make it plausible to ascribe sickness to them. They are said to be greedy for meat, to want their neighbours to die so that they can share the funeral feast. But they do not wait for this to happen. They can mysteriously consume the entrails of the living; hence the feeling of weakness that a sick person has. And since nobody has ever seen a witch engaged in this vampire activity, they must be able to make themselves invisible; and since suspected witches are not commonly observed to be away from their homes at night, their spirits must be able to leave their bodies and fly through the air to the homes of their victims.

There is no conclusive refutation of the belief in witchcraft, since whatever explanation one can give in scientific terms of impersonal causes, the question always remains 'Why me? Why just then?'. All sick persons do not die; all persons exposed to an infection do not catch it; half a dozen people went up the ladder before it slipped and this one broke his neck. And some people fall off ladders and do not break their necks. In Europe we answer these questions by talking about chance, or, if we are more superstitious, luck. The Chinese include the idea of luck among the forces governing the universe; but they do not regard luck as uncontrollable. They have worked out elaborate ways of discovering when the time is lucky for any enterprise they are interested in and so protecting themselves against ill-luck.

What is particularly interesting about the beliefs attaching to witchcraft in Africa, where they are more prevalent and more highly elaborated than at the present time in other continents, is their close association with the idea that people should not suffer unjustly. This idea has presented a puzzle to all those persons – the majority – who believe that the universe is divinely ordered: that prosperity is, or should be, earned by right conduct. The ancestors in most African societies are thought to be concerned that their descendants should live in amity together, the juniors giving respect and obedience to the seniors. They may intervene, it is believed, to punish people who depart from these principles, or on their own account to remind their descendants of their duty to offer sacrifices. But it is not only disrespectful young people who fall sick; indeed, for obvious reasons, old and respected people often do. The world is not wholly just, then; we face the problem of evil or unmerited suffering.

Explanations of evil

Different cosmologies deal with this in different ways. When Reo Fortune was on the small island of Dobu in the New Guinea archipelago, the whole male population of the village where he lived was engaged in making sorcery spells against their neighbours; this was a matter of fact, not fantasy.[1] There was no lack of explanation there when something went wrong, and no need to invoke the anger of dead ancestors or other spirits.

On Manus, in the Admiralty Islands, where Fortune also worked, unmerited sickness or death was ascribed to malicious ghosts. Ghosts in general were believed to be ill-disposed towards the living. But every household had a compact with one particular ghost, that of a kinsman recently dead, whose skull was preserved in the rafters and who protected the inhabitants from the malice of the others as long as they kept to the very strict rules of Manus morality.[2] Other Melanesian peoples believe in spirits who are angered by particular offences, but do not suppose that all suffering should be punishment, and explain it by the sorcery of humans or the caprice of non-human beings.[3]

One or two African peoples believe in a kind of anti-god, or rather a dark manifestation of god – not an independent adversary like the Ahriman of the Persians. The Lugbara of western Uganda are among these.[4] Their 'bad god' does not make it unnecessary for them to ascribe their troubles to witchcraft, but they fear him, they picture him as like a man sliced vertically down the middle, they think he is the ultimate cause of death, though he may use witches and sorcerers as his agents. The Dinka of the southern Sudan have a 'black god', Macardit ('the great black one'), who, like witches, as I shall show later, is associated with the uncultivated bush where there is no moral or social order. He is the final explanation of misfortunes which cannot be interpreted as deserved punishments; but since to accept a disaster as the work of Macardit means accepting it as irremediable, Dinka do ascribe misfortunes to witches also. But as I shall be arguing later, what people do when they think they are being bewitched is only loosely connected with their theoretical ideas about witches.

Among the adherents of world religions, Buddhists ascribe their misfortunes to unidentifiable transgressions in a forgotten previous incarnation. The Chinese have a very wide variety of explanations of misfortune, in which witchcraft does not play an important part. Since the time of the Book of Job, Jews and then Christians have believed that a just God might let his servants suffer to test the strength of their faith.

The witchcraft explanation rests on the boundless possibilities of sheer human malevolence; it is easily acceptable because we all know the depths of our own hearts. Who has never said 'You'll be sorry one day' or 'I wish you were dead'? Although few well-educated city-dwellers would ascribe a sudden attack of lumbago to a rival in some field of competition, there are equally few who will genuinely accept their own inadequacy as the reason for the greater success of their rivals; we prefer to blame it on 'prejudice' or even 'jealousy', with the assumption that our superiority is actually plain to those who refuse to grant it overt recognition. People talk of 'jealousy' in the most improbable contexts – for example, to account for adverse press notices of a theatrical performance, though the critics are in no sense competitors of the actors. Is this so much less irrational than the belief that you can kill an enemy by hating him?

Sources of supernatural harm

Of course the witch's hatred is not the only possible explanation of suffering caused by what I shall find it convenient to call 'mystical' means. In societies where the belief in non-human beings who can affect humans is strong, there are various ways in which humans may be supposedly able to harness the power the spirits wield. Some humans may be thought to have mystical power in their own right. The weapon that such persons most commonly wield is the curse; and in African belief a curse is a way of asserting authority and not just an expression of ill-will. The elders of kin groups are often believed to have this power. So may certain persons who have ritual authority over others than their own junior kin; for example, the Leopard Skin Priests among the Nuer of the southern Sudan. These men, who are so called because they wear short cloaks of leopard skin, have the responsibility of restoring peace after a homicide has led to a feud (a demand for revenge and a rupture of relations) between the kin of the slain man and those of the killer. The priest cannot force them to make up their quarrel; he can persuade the injured side to accept compensation in cattle, but when the feuding parties meet to discuss this, honour demands that the slain man's kin make a great show of being unwilling to forgo revenge. If this goes on too long, the priest may threaten to curse them for their refusal to make peace. Many African peoples believe that certain of one's relatives can, if they are provoked, curse one with very dreadful consequences, and therefore must be treated with especial respect. For example, the rule that the children of women of one's lineage or clan have an especially strong claim on one, which is universal in patrilineal African societies, is sometimes reinforced by the belief that a 'sister's son' who is ill-treated can curse his 'mother's brother' so that food will never cook again on his fire. It will be seen that in all these cases the belief is that mystical powers can be brought in on the side of right.

When we speak of a curse we imply that words are spoken in the presence of the person threatened with mystical retribution. A more subtle method, and one which is rather exceptional, consists in privately seeking the aid of the ancestors against someone who offends against accepted rules of amity among kinsmen and respect for seniority. This is called 'invocation', and has been treated most fully in John Middleton's *Lugbara Religion*, which describes a people living on the Uganda-Congo border. The Lugbara are organised into small lineages (a lineage consists of persons who reckon common descent either in the paternal or the maternal line; the Lugbara are patrilineal). Each of these recognises an elder who is the moral authority over the junior members and their wives. If he is offended, whether by disrespect to himself or by some other breach of the rules of amity and good behaviour, he goes to the shrine of his dead forbears, of which he is custodian, and sits there thinking of his indignation. The ghosts, it is believed, hear his unspoken thoughts and punish the guilty person; that is, some time later when the culprit falls sick, this will be revealed as the cause.

Somewhat similar are the ideas of the Nyakyusa, who live in the interior of Tanzania, at the upper end of Lake Nyasa. They believe that when a person does something that shocks his neighbours, they will begin to murmur about it, and the cold breath of their whispers will chill him and make him sick.

All these ideas belong to the field of legitimate action against misbehaviour. In some circumstances one might include in this field the use of magic – charms and spells and objects believed to have mystical power. In the language of anthropologists harmful magic is generally called sorcery, and most sorcery is thought to be illegitimate. But it is possible in Africa to buy from a sorcerer protective magic which will keep thieves off your property, and in parts of New Guinea different families are believed to own different kinds of harmful magic with which they protect their own food crops. It is also possible in Africa, after something has been stolen, to get a sorcerer to make magic which will injure the unknown thief if he does not make restitution; an interesting variant of this idea comes from the Nyoro of western Uganda, who have medicine to smear on the ruins of a house that has been burnt down, so as to punish the person responsible. The chiefs of the Trobriand Islands in New Guinea were generally supposed to employ sorcerers against anyone who threatened their authority.

Witchcraft in contrast is unambiguously evil. It may well be motivated; it is often ascribed to the ill-feeling generated in some quarrel, which is remembered when one of the parties falls sick or meets with some other misfortune. But it is always held to be unjustified; the witch may have had good cause for anger, but if he had not had an evil disposition he would not have expressed his anger in this way. It follows, of course, that the anger of a witch is by definition not 'righteous anger'.

The moral line which divides these ways of giving practical effect to hostile feelings is not as sharp as this account might suggest. Who is to judge whether an expression of anger is that of a righteous upholder of authority or of a peevish old man? The person to whom others ascribe a 'bad disposition', an 'evil heart', or whatever the metaphor may be, probably does not admit to it himself. If he is always in quarrels it is because other people quarrel with him. The ambiguous, and in a sense non-committal, phrase 'We shall see' or 'You will see', taken to imply a threat of witchcraft in many parts of Africa, may also convey a legitimate curse. Real-life suspicions and accusations of witchcraft or sorcery are matters of public opinion. But in systems of ideas, in generalised descriptions, there is a sharp distinction between the person for whose activities there may be some justification and the one for whom there can be none. The latter, in most societies, is the witch.

Witches and sorcerers

It may be too late now to recreate from historical records a detailed picture of a community in Europe where the belief in witchcraft was an active force: to trace out the relationship between accused witches and their accusers, and find just what events were most frequently ascribed to witchcraft and what the persons accused had done to invite the enmity of the accuser or general public hostility, to see what actually happened when an individual was accused, and

Horns used in divination by
the Kuba of the Congo (Kinshasa).
Sometimes the horn is supposed to
speak to its owner.

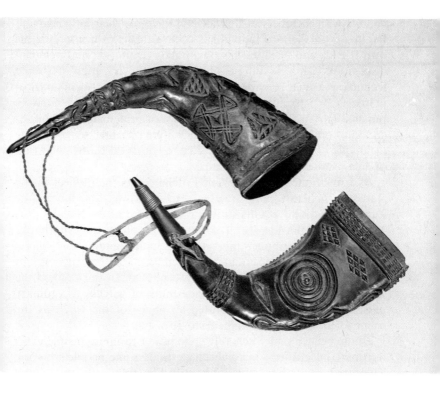

how often those who were supposedly convicted were put to death
or otherwise cruelly treated, during all the centuries before witchcraft began to be equated with heresy. To see the process of misfortune, suspicion, accusation and public reaction in its social
setting, as one, albeit a dramatic one, of the incidents of everyday
life, the enquirer must go to a society where witchcraft is still taken
for granted as a causal explanation; and he must live in close

contact with members of this society, speaking their language and familiar with them as individuals each with his own interests, his own friends and enemies, his own public reputation and personal disposition. This is still possible among the societies of simple technology which provide the main field of study of social anthropologists. Up to now this kind of study has been most actively pursued in Africa, and it has been pursued principally by English-speaking anthropologists, since they were the first to adopt the technique of 'participant observation' as opposed to the collection of data by questioning informants.

As I mentioned earlier, Evans-Pritchard was the pioneer in the study of witchcraft by this method. His work was done among the Zande of the Bahr-el-Ghazal in the south west of the Sudan.[5] It is a paradox in the history of social anthropology that the books which have contributed most to our understanding of general principles of social behaviour have been based on the experience of societies which later proved to be exceptional. In this context the Zande are exceptional because they think of witches as ordinary persons, and have not elaborated an image of the witch as the enemy of all good men and the epitome of evil.

Zande believe that witchcraft – the power to injure people without material means – is a substance inside some people's bodies. They are born with it; a man inherits his from his father, a woman from her mother. No one can know whether someone has this substance unless his body is opened after he dies; least of all do the possessors of it know. Anyone may be a witch, therefore; and the witchcraft can operate without the intention of its possessor. Zande witches, then, are not the objects of severe moral judgments, nor thought to be set apart as a special kind of being. The Zande attitude will have to be considered further when we discuss what people do when they think they have been bewitched.

Zande appear to be rather exceptional in the extent to which witchcraft occupies their thoughts, although this need not be taken to imply that they are haunted by constant fears, any more than westerners are perpetually weighed down by the dread of nuclear warfare, though most of us think about it sometimes. The accounts of anthropologists suggest that most people begin to think seriously about witchcraft when disaster has struck, though some pray to the ancestors to protect them from witches, some have institutions designed periodically to rid the community of witches, and individuals may become very frightened if they see some object that they associate with the doings of witches. Zande protect themselves in advance, as well as they can, by the consultation of oracles which supposedly tell them if they are in danger from it, when they plan an expedition for example.

Evans-Pritchard gives the following list of events which might be ascribed to witchcraft:

If blight seizes the groundnut crop it is witchcraft; if the bush is vainly scoured for game it is witchcraft; if termites do not rise when their swarming is due and a cold useless night is spent in waiting for their flight it is witchcraft; if a wife is sulky and unresponsive to her husband it is witchcraft; if a prince is cold and distant with his subject it is witchcraft; if a magical rite fails to achieve its purpose it is witchcraft; if, in fact, any failure or misfortune falls upon anyone at any time and in relation to any of the manifold activities of his life it may be due to witchcraft.[6]

Not many peoples have been found to ascribe such a variety of events to this cause.

A number of other peoples on the left bank of the Congo share this belief in witchcraft as an inborn physical quality. Such peoples make a clear distinction between witchcraft and sorcery, which operates by the manipulation of substances. A somewhat similar belief is held by the Nyakyusa, whose ideas on the chilling breath of moral disapproval have been mentioned. The Nyakyusa believe that a witch has a python in his belly, and that at night he flies

A Benin ivory carving
of the deity Orunmila who
gives power to diviners.

21

through the air, either in the form of a python or on its back, and in this guise sucks the internal substance from people as they lie asleep, or the milk from their cattle. Righteous men who are able to defend the village against witches have pythons too, which go out and do nightly battle against the witch pythons; and when the head-man of a village is installed, part of the ritual that is performed to make him able to carry out his duties well is believed to give him this mystical power of defence against witches.[7]

Although Evans-Pritchard did not offer the Zande ideas about witchcraft as a model to which other peoples should be expected to conform, many later anthropologists have leant heavily on the distinction between witchcraft and sorcery. Some have taken the whole Zande complex – physical substance, inherited, acting without the volition of its possessor – and have sought to distinguish witches from sorcerers by all three criteria. They have met the nemesis of over-definition; in the vast variety of human social life one should not expect to find three such ideas linked in very many societies, even those which fall within one geographical area. As it happens, many of the best accounts of witchcraft and sorcery beliefs and the way they are applied in practical situations come from eastern and central Africa, but no comparable studies have been made of near neighbours of the Zande. The writers of these accounts have found it difficult to separate the two types of evil-doer, and quite impossible to do so if they are to be obliged to say that witchcraft to deserve the name must be inherited, and involuntary in action; and they have also found that the peoples among whom they worked did not make a clear verbal distinction. Thus a number of Bantu languages use words built on the stem *log-*, *lok-* or *loj-* to refer without distinction to all the ways they know by which humans can cause mystical injuries.

Again, the idea of involuntary witchcraft need not be linked with the idea that it is an inherited substance. The Lunda and Luvale in

Zambia, for example, do not think anyone is born with witch-craft inside him, but some women are believed to have spirit familiars who bring them riches and demand in return human lives, in the taking of which the owner of the familiar has no direct interest. The familiar may kill its owner if it is not gratified with another life. When the owner dies it is believed to attach itself to her daughter or sister, a woman who has no desire for such a relationship. The Ndembu, also in Zambia, believe that a man cannot inflict mystical harm without the use of medicines, but that evil men also have spirit familiars who may do their killing for them. Such men have the qualities of both sorcerer and witch, and indeed they may create their own familiars out of the blood of their victims. Women, the Ndembu think, also have familiars, of a different and more dangerous kind; they demand the lives of their owner's kin, and though they may be refused three times, after that they kill as they please. Here too the familiar is believed to attach itself to a daughter or sister when its owner dies. Other peoples believe that witches learn their trade – whatever it is – from their parents.

What I myself would regard as the essential characteristic of a witch, the evil disposition that at least theoretically sets him outside the pale of common humanity, is lacking in the beliefs of the Zande themselves. Many other peoples, including the Nyakyusa, do draw this picture of the witch as the anti-model of approved behaviour. But the Lugbara say that sorcerers – in the sense of people who use medicines – are more evil than witches who use only the emotions of anger and envy.

So it is impossible to specify that only persons with a particular combination of qualities are to be called witches; the name would have no usefulness. Some would prefer to drop the name, or to use the terms 'sorcery' or 'witchcraft' indiscriminately, or to invent some new word that would subsume all the characteristics that have

This Pondo man has the reputation of being a sorcerer. By profession he was a purveyor of African medicines. He can be seen to be prosperous, and was by no means ostracised. Persons who were invited to comment on him said it was no good trying to avoid witches and sorcerers, there were too many.

been associated with both. I would suggest that, even if it is rarely practicable to divide supposed evil-doers sharply into witches and sorcerers, it is still useful to distinguish types of evil-doing on these lines. The distinction I would make is a simple one – that the sorcerer uses material objects and the witch does not. It is by no means insignificant, since it is possible to find evidence of sorcery, and indeed many objects used for that purpose have been found when people are accused, when people make voluntary confessions, and in Europe sometimes in old abandoned houses. But there can never be evidence of witchcraft, and so accusations of witchcraft can only be pursued by means as mystical as the supposed offence.

Another reason for keeping apart the idea of causing harm by one's mere disposition and that of causing harm by the use of materials – even though many peoples do not regard these as the attributes of different types of person – is that those who have knowledge of the properties of materials may know how to use them for the benefit of their fellows, and particularly to cure disease. An anthropologist would today use the term 'magic' to cover this combined field. One can certainly distinguish between the social and anti-social uses of magic, though I have already mentioned the possibility that harmful magic may be employed for purposes that are socially approved. If one person is held to possess the whole range of magical knowledge there is no objective way of deciding whether he should be called a magician (good) or a sorcerer (usually bad). Where he will be classed by his fellows will be a matter of circumstances. Persons who hold ritual offices – the rainmaker, the Leopard Skin Priest, the custodians of temples of dead kings, the *laibon* whose blessing was required before the Masai warriors set out on a raid – are generally assumed to be good. Yet rainmakers may be suspected of manipulating the weather to damage their enemies, and the *laibon* is feared as coming from a line of powerful sorcerers. More ambiguous is the position of the man who claims defensive powers against sorcerers or witches; how could he know how to deal with them if he were not one of them? Such suspicions may be harboured even against the supposedly neutral diviners who are called in to identify the cause of a sickness.

The earliest Roman law made magic a crime. But what was this crime? Apparently the causing of harm to others, but not other ways of exercising supposedly mystical powers. The Roman world possessed a great body of pseudo-medical lore in which materials were used according to the principles of what James Frazer in *The Golden Bough* taught us to call sympathetic magic. But to the

Romans this was accepted wisdom, not magic. Magic came into the picture if the practitioner was supposed to have acquired his knowledge by occult means, and particularly through the power of foretelling the future. The famous second-century physician, Galen, was accused of practising magic because of his accuracy in predicting the course of a disease ('uncanny', his rivals thought it). Galen himself, reasoning much as we do today, dismissed as 'magical' the treatments that he did not believe in, enumerating among them prescriptions to make people barren, or strike them dumb when they were defending themselves in court. There were, of course, in the Roman empire many purveyors of spells who did not profess to have medical knowledge.

In early Christian days magicians were believed to get their power from demons or evil spirits – not yet the Devil who was later to be thought of as the master and consort of witches. Christian authorities distinguished magic from miracles, which were the work of God through particularly holy men. Prayers to God – sometimes answered by miracles – took the place in Christianity of such activities as the rainmaking rituals of paganism, and relics of the saints in the custody of church authorities had the wonder-working powers of the magician's medicines. The word magician in those days implied the claim to foresee the future through horoscopes as did the eastern Magi, and this was thought to be both fraudulent and subversive, since it could lead to speculations on the death of persons in high places. Apuleius, the author of *The Golden Ass*, when he was put on trial for practising magic, remarked that the Magi were priests in their own country, and this brings home the point that an activity which in one context has all the sanction of authority may be treated as a crime if it is practised without this authority. In rural England practitioners of folk medicine were sometimes called 'white witches', with the implication that they got their knowledge, beneficial as it was, from illicit sources, and if they were suspected

Ein erschröckliche geschicht/so zu Derneburg in der Graffschafft Reinsteyn/am Hartz gelegen/von dreyen Zauberin/vnnd zwayen Mañen/Jñ etlichen tagen des Monats Octobris Jm 1555. Jare ergangen ist.

DJe alte Schlang der Teüffel/dieweyl er Got/vnd zůuoran den Sun Gottes/vnsern Herrn Jesum Christum/vnd das gantze menschliche geschlecht/fürnemlich vmb vnsers Haylands Christi willen hasset/hat er sich bald im anfang/vnd kürtzlich nach der erschaffung vmb dz weibß bild/als vmb die/welcher same seinen kopff zertretten solt/angenomẽ/dieselbigen durch sein hinderlist vnd lugen/zů dem jämerlichen fal/deß vnglaubens vñ vngehorsams wider Got gebracht/Darauß das gantz menschlich geschlecht/in ewige verdamnuß vñ verderben komen were/so Christus vnser Hayland/den zorn des Vatters nicht weckgenomen/vnd das gericht wider vns auffgehaben het. Nu behelt der alte Feind gleichwol alten haß wider Christum/vnd vns/für vñ für/vnd helt auch sein alte weyse/er setzet sonderlich dem weiblichen gschlecht hart zů/als dem schwecheren werckzeug/damit er sie von Christo wegreysse/vñ in ewige verdamnuß füre/vñ wie er zů Eua sprach/sie wurden werdẽ wie die Götter/Also bläßt er noch das gifft in der weyber hertzen/lernet sie zaubern/auff das er sie klůg mache/das sie mehr wissen dann andere leüt/vnd also den Göttern gleich werden/damit macht er sie jm anhengig/vnd zů Teüffels dienerin/ja auch zů Teuffels breüten/wie dise jämerliche geschicht/welche warhafftigklich also wie vnden angezaiget/am Hartz ergangen ist/Die derhalben also gemalet vñ geschriben/im druck auß gangen. Auff das doch die rohe lose welt/zů Gottes forcht erwecket/vnd von dem Gottlosen wesen abgeschreckt werden/ Dann Gott der allmächtige derhalben solche Exempel vns sehen laßt/das er damit vnsere harten hertzen durch dise erschröckliche exempel / zur forcht Göttliches gerichts/vnd straffe erwecke/man mag es malen/predigen/singen vnd sagen/vñ wie man jmer kan den leüten einbilden/damit der laydige hauffe ein wenig zů Gottes forcht/gehorsam/vnd zucht gezogen werde/besonder zů disen letsten zeyten/in welchẽ der listige Sathan/dieweyl er mercket/das der tag des gerichts sich nahet/gar rassend toll vnd vnsinnig ist/vnd bede durch sich vnd seine gelider/grewlicher weyse/wider Christum vnd sein armes heüfflein wüttet/Die ellende welt aber dargegẽ so frey sicher in allem můtwillen dahin lebet/als ob der Teüffel vor langst gestorben sey/vnd kain Got/kain gericht oder straff/verhanden were/Der Almächtig Got vnd vatter/vnsers Herrn Jesu Christi/wölle dem grimigen feinde wehren/sein armes heüfflein vor jm vnd seinen glidern schützen vnd handthaben/seinem vnd der seinen wütten vnd toben/einmal ein ende machen/durch Jesum Christum Amen.

¶ Folget die geschichte / so zů Derneburg in der Graffschafft Reynstein am Hartz gelegen/ergangen ist/ Jm October des 1555. Jars.

AVff den Dinstag nach Michaelis/den ersten Octobris/seind zwů Zauberin gebrandt/die eine Gröbische/die ander Gißlersche genañt/ vñ hat die Gröbische bekandt/das sie Aylff jar mit dem Teüffel gebůlet habe/vñ wie man dieselben Gröbischen zů der Fewrstat gebracht/vnd an die saul mit Ketten geschlagen/vnd das Fewr angezündt/ist der bůle/der Sathan komen/vnd sie in lüfften sichtigklich vor yederman weckgefürt. Am Donerstag/nach dem die Gröbische vñ die Gißlerschin am Dinstag zůuor seind gerichtet worden/das ist den 3. Octobris/seind dise bede Frawen auff den abend in der Gißlersche hauß komen/vnd der Gißlerschen man zur thür hinauß gestossen/das er nider gefallen vnnd gestorben ist/welches ain Nachbaur gegen vber gehöret/vnd zů gelauffen ist/durch die thür gesehen/das zway weyber bede eytel fewrige/vmbs fewr gedantzet/der Gißlerschin man aber/lag vor der thür vnd war todt. Am Sonnabendt nach Dionisij/das ist der 12. Octobris/ist der Gröbischen mañ gerichtet worden/vmb der vrsach willẽ/das er bey seines weybs schwester geschlaffen hat/welche er zůuorn zum weybe gehabt/vñ darnach die Gröbischen genomẽ/Des Montags darnach/das ist der 14. Octobris ist ain weyb die Serckschen genandt/auch verbrandt worden/der vrsach/das sie des Herrn Achacius von Veldthaym des Stiffts Halberstat Hauptmañs weybe vergeben hate/ vnd ainem mañ zů Derneburg ain Krotten vnter die Schwöllen gegraben/daruon der man erlamet/vnd jm das vihe vmbkomen ist.

¶ Hie sihet man wañ der Teüffel an ainem orth einnistet/vñ begundt zů Regieren/wie wüst er mit seinem gifft vmb sich stichet/wie vil personen komen hie vmb/in wenig tagen/vnd soll vns solch grewlich exempel billich raytzen zur bůß/vnd zur forcht Gottes/auff das wir vns mit dem wort Gottes vnd gebette/wider den gemelten feynd schützen/vnd mag dise Historj den sichern gotlosen Epicurern vnnd Zaubrern/wol ain erinnerung sein/dieweyl sie sehen/das der Teüffel noch lebt/vnd das daß Hellische fewr noch nit erloschen ist/Der Almechtig Got wölle sie auch zur bůsse bringen/vnd vns alle inn/vnd bey seinem raynen wort erhalten/vnd mit seinem hayligen Gayst regieren/ auff das wir leben inn aller Gottseligkayt/Zucht vnd Erbarkayt/zů ehren seinem hayligen Namen/Durch vnsern Herren Jesum Christum/ AMEN.

¶ Getruckt zů Nürnberg bey Jörg Merckel/durch verleg Endres Zenckel Botten.

A sixteenth-century broadsheet
describing the burning of three
witches, one of whom was rescued
by the Devil, in Regenstein
in the Harz mountains.

27

of harming others it was explicitly said to come from the devil. But it was only during the centuries of persecution which the German scholar Hansen called the 'witch-madness' (*Zauberwahn*) that it became official doctrine to link witches with the Devil. Now witches, who had made a compact with the Devil and promised to serve him, were distinguished from sorcerers, who had learnt their arts from him but remained free agents in the practice of it.

The witches of Europe were not thought to achieve their ends by evil wishes alone, far from it. The evidence at their trials is concerned as much with their familiars and the objects found in their homes as with the supposed physical marks imprinted on them by the Devil. But they are depicted as being in their actions and dispositions everything that was most abhorred by the society of that time. In this respect the image of the witch as it is presented in the writings of the fifteenth to seventeenth centuries parallels the image of the witch as it is described in the folk-lore of non-literate peoples. The striking difference between European and contemporary believers in witches is that the former sought to prove that real human beings conformed to the image. In both contexts the accused person is a neighbour whom everyone knows. But the accusers in Africa today are content to ascribe some particular injury to his witchcraft or sorcery; they do not also seek to prove that his whole life violates every decency. What Trevor-Roper says of the Roman attitude applies to Africa too:

Punishment could only be inflicted for harm done by witchcraft; merely to 'be' a witch was not enough.

Questions to be considered

This book will be mainly concerned with the ideas and practices of the peoples who today take the existence of witchcraft for granted. Such peoples can be found in most parts of the world, although the

Modern Africa, showing
principal tribes mentioned
in the text.

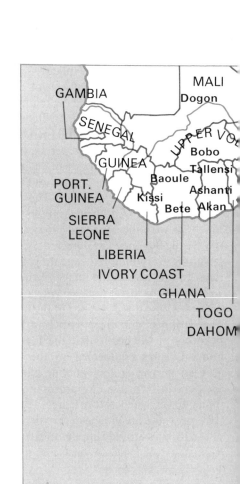

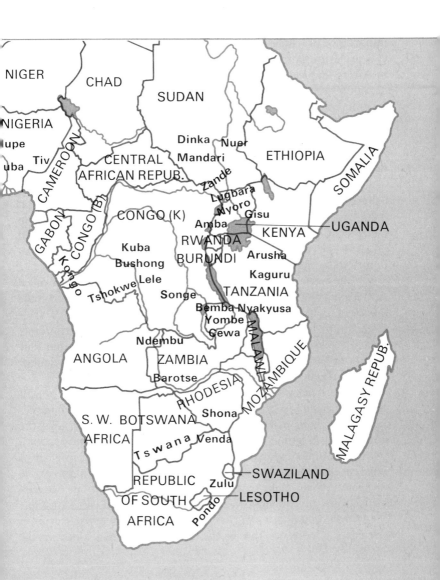

importance of witches in their scheme of things varies very widely. It is in Africa that they are of the greatest significance, because it is in Africa that the idea that suffering is inflicted by spiritual beings as a punishment is most highly developed. An explanation of misfortune which lays the blame on the sufferer is too hard for most people to accept. It has to be softened by the possibility that some suffering is undeserved, and this is where the belief in witchcraft is invoked. This is why Monica Wilson, writing of an East African people, said that it was impossible to make a study of their religion which did not include witchcraft. Many peoples in other continents believe in the existence of witches and will tell you stories about them, but if they believe that their sufferings come either from malevolent spirits or from sorcerers whose activity is no more and no less to be condemned than physical fighting, they are not driven to turn to witchcraft as an explanation of actual events.

It is however in Africa, and particularly in eastern and central Africa, that the anthropologists of the last thirty years have made the most detailed observations, not only of ideas but of their application: how witches are imagined, what people do to protect themselves against witches, on what grounds they decide that they have been bewitched, what action they take then, and in particular, how they decide whom to accuse.

Evans-Pritchard's work among the Zande has been mentioned. Three other full-length books deal with Zambia and Rhodesia. Turner's *Schism and Continuity in an African Society* tells the story of an Ndembu village on the Angola border and traces a series of dramas involving the same set of characters, in each of which accusations of witchcraft were made. Marwick's *Sorcery in its Social Setting* seeks to establish statistical correlations between accusations of witchcraft and particular social relationships. Crawford's *Witchcraft and Sorcery in Rhodesia* uses material from law cases and places this in the context of Shona ideas on the subject. Monica Wilson writing on Nyakyusa religion, and Middleton on that of the Lugbara, found that the subject could not be made intelligible without a discussion of witchcraft. Most people who have done field-work in Africa have brought back some information on the subject.

No French writer has yet devoted a volume to problems of witchcraft in Africa, and French ethnographers have on the whole been more interested in generalised statements of social rules and cosmological theories than in events which illustrate the relevance of belief in its social setting. An exception is Denise Paulme, whose observations among the Bete of the Ivory Coast are referred to in chapter 8. She has recorded the experiences of Africans who, as they thought, had been tricked into becoming witches, and of one who was indignant at the injustice of trial by ordeal, and has herself witnessed and photographed the dances of diviners who claimed to identify witches. She has also recorded the sorcery beliefs of the Kissi in the interior of Guinea (*Les Gens du Riz*, 1954). The real or supposed medical effects of magic both for harming and curing were studied in the Ivory Coast and Upper Volta by J. Kerharo and A. Bousquet (*Sorciers, Féticheurs et Guérisseurs*, 1950).

A collection of statements on witchcraft and sorcery beliefs of the Bobo of Upper Volta, made and translated by a French doctor, J. Cremer, who died in Africa in 1920, was edited and published by H. Labouret, and is of interest in that it presents in their own words the ideas of informants who had not yet learned to conceal beliefs that Europeans despise (*Les Bobo, Mentalité Mystique*, 1927). Another older book which discussed sorcery and witch beliefs at some length is L. Tauxier, *La Religion Bambara* (1924).

Outside Africa the only full-length book is Kluckhohn's *Navaho Witchcraft*, which is a collection of statements by informants that are hard to interpret adequately unless one already knows a good deal about the Navaho Indians of the south-western United States.

The books on witchcraft in western Europe, in England and in colonial America have nearly all been written by people who did not look for parallels to contemporary witch beliefs outside Europe, if they knew that these existed. Most of the writers have been interested rather in asking why persons in high authority persecuted witches than in asking what ordinary people did about them. One of them, Margaret Murray, advanced a theory of the Black Mass and the compact with the Devil that was specifically related to the history of Europe and had no general applicability. Although this book is primarily concerned with contemporary ideas, I shall try to see how far European witch beliefs can be related with what anthropologists think about Africa.

2 What are witches like ?

Evans-Pritchard's study of Zande ideas about witches and their ways was followed by Monica Wilson's work on the Nyakyusa, who, as has been mentioned, make the same distinction between witches and sorcerers as the Zande do. Monica Wilson had already made an anthropological study of the Pondo in the Cape Province of South Africa, and was struck by the differences in the beliefs of these two peoples about witches. In summing up a comparison between them, she wrote 'I see witch beliefs as the standardised nightmares of a group',[1] and she suggested that further research should throw light on the reasons for different kinds of nightmare.

The analogy of the nightmare is a good one; it describes the kind of terror that is not ever-present but becomes conscious when people are in anxiety or distress. Moreover, people do dream of witches, and among the Nyakyusa this is thought to be a reliable way of identifying them. In a mental hospital in Zambia a number of patients, given paint and paper, made pictures of the human-headed serpents who the Ndembu and their neighbours think are the familiars of sorcerers.

Monica Wilson, however, was concerned less with the nightmare quality of witch beliefs than with the fact that they are standardised for different societies. People do not have their private visions of witches; they recognise that what their dream shows them is a witch because they have been taught what a witch is like.

Monica Wilson observed that Nyakyusa and Pondo had quite different ideas about the characteristics and activities of witches. For Nyakyusa the most significant thing about them was their greed for food, which led them to feast on the internal organs of their sleeping neighbours and suck dry the milk of their cattle; and because they were believed to consume their neighbours in this way, it was natural to ascribe sickness to them. Nyakyusa witches might be of either sex. Pondo witches, on the other hand, were women who had sex relations with familiar spirits, and these

Pondo homesteads, each some distance from its neighbours. Monica Wilson believes that Pondo ideas of the characteristics and behaviour of witches are connected with this form of settlement. A Pondo homestead is the home of people who are all kin, and people are in close contact with forbidden sexual partners. But they do not envy others' wealth, because the property of the homestead belongs to all its members.

spirits were believed to be light in colour. She explains these differences by reference to the different structure of the two societies. The Nyakyusa, alone among the African peoples we know, live in villages of unrelated men of the same age, with their wives; the Pondo, more typically, live in large family homesteads, a man and his wives, his sons and their wives, together. A family homestead is a property-owning unit; its cattle belong to it as a group, and although members may resent the way they are allocated, it would be meaningless to speak of one section envying the wealth of another. In a village of unrelated men some may be rich, some poor (relatively); and no one can help knowing when a richer neighbour is roasting the meat of a sacrifice. Monica Wilson makes much of the fact that Nyakyusa speak of witches *smelling* roasting meat. Nyakyusa nightmares, she argues, are focused on the envy of wealth.

Pondo, she continues, usually interpret sickness as a punishment from the ancestors and deal with it by sacrifice. But their nightmares are sexual, for two reasons. One is that the rules prohibiting sex relations between persons related by descent are very extensive, and that in the Pondo homestead people are in constant contact with prohibited partners. The other is that in South Africa sex relations between persons of different races are severely condemned; at the time when Pondo witch beliefs were formed they were not penalised by law as they are now. Hence, Monica Wilson argues, the emphasis on the light-coloured familiars of women witches.

At about the same time the late Frederick Nadel,[2] working in northern Nigeria, found that the Nupe of Ilorin province had an elaborate idea of an organisation of women witches led by the recognised head of the women traders, a real, identifiable person. He explained this belief by the fact that Nupe women are so successful at trading that their husbands are often dependent on them financially, and understandably resent this. Peter Morton-Williams,[3] writing of the south-western Yoruba, tells us that they too believe that witches are always women and that they direct their witchcraft against their husbands and children. Here too women are traders, but it seems to be much less common for them to make themselves economically independent, and there is no question of seeing the witches' coven as the nocturnal counterpart of the market-women's guild. Indeed, Morton-Williams offers quite a different explanation for Yoruba notions about witchcraft. He says it is suspected particularly when children die, in this area with a forty per cent infant mortality rate; husbands suspect their wives, women their co-wives or their mothers-in-law.

The universal image of the witch

These explanations of different types of witch belief are interesting, but anthropologists have not developed this line of inquiry very far. It does not seem that specific beliefs can be seen as characteristic of particular kinds of society, and it is perhaps equally interesting to see what there is in common in the image of the witch that is current in different parts of the world.

If the Pondo do not think witches are greedy for meat, this is certainly interesting, but many peoples who live in family home-steads do, the Lugbara of western Uganda, for example. The Ndembu of Zambia believe that a woman's familiar may kill her husband. If she does, his ghost becomes an even more dangerous being, the leader of the non-human familiars. He is believed to have intercourse with his widow and to give her inordinate plea-sure. But the bands of witches and familiars gather together for the purpose of eating the bodies of their victims. The greed motif and the sexual motif are combined, and I should be inclined to say this is more usual. A high infant mortality rate is characteristic of all those parts of the world that lack medical knowledge and skills. Every society which believes in witches certainly does have its nightmare figure, and usually some additional notions about the kind of people who are likely to be witches. In actual cases, where a disaster is ascribed to witchcraft, and an accusation must be pinned on someone, theory is not necessarily brought to bear; real accusations are matters of personal enmity and not of evidence of witch-like behaviour. In this respect African attitudes towards witches differ from those that guided the most famous witch-trials of Europe and colonial America, to the advantage of Africa.

If beliefs about the nightmare witch are found to have much in common all over the world, this is surely to be explained by the fact that the bases of social order are common; respect for life and property and for the rules governing sexual behaviour. The night-mare witch is the being that flouts those rules and in addition dis-regards the standards of decency that every society, however simple, thinks of as making it 'civilised' in contrast to real or imagined 'savages' outside. He (as often as she) embodies every conception of evil of which his creators are capable.

The nightmare witch is often explicitly distinguished from the everyday witch, usually by a phrase that refers to prowling at night. The everyday witch, the person who may actually be living among you, suspected or unsuspected, also embodies an antithesis – this time the antithesis of the kind of person we like our neighbours to be. Finally, certain categories of person who for one reason or another are thought to be not wholly members of the community, and so not entirely to be trusted, are described in general terms as likely to be witches; and the theories which are held about the inheritance of witchcraft may have practical significance when they can be invoked to pin suspicion on a particular individual. But the fantasy world where nightmares reign and the real world where witches are identified as the cause of misfortune do not often coincide.

In the nightmare world one finds in fact that the same types of sinister doings are ascribed to witches in places thousands of miles apart. One might say there is a basic outfit of witch activities ascribed to all, or nearly all, witches. The Navaho Indians hold, in common with many African peoples and with Roman and medieval Europe, that witches can turn themselves into animals (were-wolves) and that they gather together to feast on corpses. They share with the Zande the belief that witches can shoot into the bodies of their victims alien substances which the detectors of witchcraft can find and remove; as far as the Zande are concerned, this belief might seem to be inconsistent with the idea that the witch operates by his internal disposition alone. But there are two answers to this: in the first place, if the witch causes pieces of bone or charcoal to be in the bodies of his victims without having himself handled them, the more witch he; in the second, the belief in witchcraft, wherever it is held, contains all kinds of inconsistencies, and must contain them if it is to be applicable to every situation in which people want to invoke it. Again, the Navaho share with the Tiv in Nigeria the belief that witches make use of the bodies of their victims to increase their mystical power.

These details have been cited to show that peoples separated by thousands of miles and with very different types of subsistence and social organisation can have the same ideas about the sinister people to whom they ascribe their misfortunes. I have quoted beliefs which would not be found in every people's ideas of witchcraft. But a much greater number are common to most of the bodies of witch-beliefs that have been recorded. The reason for this, I suggest, is a simple one. Some of the powers ascribed to witchcraft are explanatory; given the assumption that people can injure their neighbours without going near them, they describe in a 'commonsense' way how this could be done. The troubles they are supposed to be able to cause, of course, are those for which people know no remedy. But the image of the way witches behave, which is associated with the reasons why they should seek to destroy others, is an image of evil, of the antithesis of good. And since the elementary requirements of social order are everywhere the same, one should expect that there would be more resemblances than differences in different people's imaginary pictures of the witch.

A witch then is a person who does not control the impulses that good members of society must keep in check. Insatiable desire for meat and insatiable hatreds account, separately or together, for the deaths that witches cause. They also have insatiable or perverted sexual lusts. Many people think they commit incest, and must do so in order to be able to exercise their witchcraft powers; some

Navaho informants said necrophily was also required. Others believe that female witches are nymphomaniac. It is often supposed that a witch's first victim – as it were his apprentice task – must be a close kinsman. Thus witches begin by sinning against the rules of kinship, which are more specific and binding than those of neighbourliness. They have unrestrained passions of hatred and envy, which they satisfy by their crimes. But over and above their particularised evil acts, witches are thought to behave in ways that offend the accepted decencies without doing harm to anyone in particular. It is significant, in fact, that, although the supposedly most heinous kind of witch, in Africa often distinguished by the term 'night-witch', is the one who behaves in this outrageous manner, nobody tries to show that a person accused of actually injuring someone by witchcraft is this kind of witch.

The peoples whose conceptions of the night-witch have been most fully described by anthropologists are the Dinka of the southern Sudan and the Lugbara of western Uganda; although these two peoples are not closely related in language or culture, the imaginary pictures they draw are strikingly similar. The association of witches with night already separates them from normal people, who go about their avocations openly, in the light of day. Then they are associated with the bush, the uncultivated land outside the homestead or village, on which man has not imposed his social order. Most of the wild animals of the bush are thought of by one people or another as the allies of witches. In these two examples witches are associated with animals which are black, disgusting, dangerous, or active at night-time. For the Lugbara the list is toad, snake, lizard, water frog, jackal, leopard, bat, owl, and a kind of monkey that screeches at night.[4] The Dinka associate witches with hyenas and, in particular, with black cobras, the most dangerous of African snakes.[5] They believe that a witch smears the blood of a black cobra on the house-posts of his victim, while their

Devi Krishna, the witch in the Balinese Barong play.
There is no reason why she should be represented as
so very old, but an aged witch satisfies the popular
imagination. When Beryl de Zoete saw this performance,
the part of the witch was played by a man.

neighbours the Mandari say the witch uses his own blood.[6] Gisu witches employ rats, sending them in pairs to collect their victims' hair or nail-clippings for use in what Frazer called homoeopathic magic; and Kaguru witches send anteaters to burrow under the walls of the victim's hut.

Witches excrete and vomit in the smooth space before the homestead which its owners keep swept and clean – sometimes even inside the house; this may be thought of as a means of bewitching as well as a symbolically outrageous action. The Mandari believe that witches steal objects and rub them with excrement as a means of harming the owner. Lugbara witches are believed to dance naked – again violating the rule that a civilised person should be clothed – and Mandari witches dance on their victims' graves, a form of sacrilege. Dancing naked is a way in which many societies conceive the ultimate outrage. I learned from the Ganda of dreadful people called Basezi who danced naked and feasted on corpses, people in whom the neighbouring Nyoro also believe, and in Malawi an African clerk of the Ngoni people, who in that area had made themselves overlords of the indigenous Cewa, told me that he had stumbled on secret rites of the Cewa and 'they were dancing naked!' Beidelman[7] was told similar stories by the Kaguru of Tanzania, some of whom even said they had seen their own close kin among the dancers. In Bunyoro, the Basezi are believed to cause death to any who see them, so that their existence remains a pure article of faith.[8] Dinka witches are thought to have tails, a characteristic which differentiates them from men and aligns them with other animals; one is reminded of the medieval image of the Devil and of the Chinese idea of Europeans.

An interesting feature of Lugbara belief is that anti-social beings – whether they are witches or merely persons outside the bounds of the recognised community – are pictured as behaving in ways that *directly* reverse the normal, notably by walking on their hands.

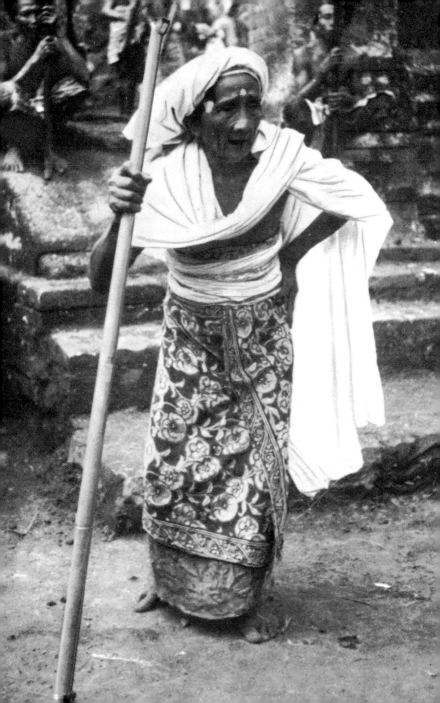

The Amba, also in western Uganda, similarly believe that witches may stand on their heads or hang by their feet from branches of trees, and that when they are thirsty they eat salt.[9] One may compare with such ideas the imaginary picture of the Witches' Sabbath or Black Mass, in which many of the reversals are thought of as deliberate profanations of what Christians hold sacred, but some, such as dancing in a ring facing outwards, merely turn the normal upside down. A striking parallel to the Amba idea is the medieval notion that witches' banquets are *without* salt.

Though when witches are accused in Africa it is always as individuals, night-witches are commonly believed to operate in groups, as they are by the Navaho. Thus one might say that the enemies of society are pictured as forming an anti-society. But in African belief the social activities of witches have not received the same imaginative elaboration as their personal characteristics. They are supposed to unite for their corpse-feasts, also sometimes to plan who their next victim shall be; it is sometimes held that every witch is expected to make a fair contribution to the total of victims. One of Kluckhohn's Navaho informants told him that a witch who had a grudge against someone would invite the help of his fellow-witches at such a gathering; and that they would be glad to help because they would all share in making 'fresh medicine' from the corpse. This kind of 'medicine' must often be as unreal as witchcraft itself, but surprising collections of objects used in sorcery have sometimes been brought to light after actual murders have been committed. In Barotseland such collections found in 1956 included concoctions said to contain human flesh.

Everyday witches

Ethnographers' accounts of the characteristics ascribed to witches link those I have just summarised with qualities that a person could in fact easily observe among his neighbours. These latter are the qualities that might cause a real person to be suspected, if not actually accused, of witchcraft. One might not expect to find all the qualities mentioned combined in the same person, but this is no disadvantage for practical purposes; it simply widens the field for suspicion and allows it to rest on more kinds of unpopular individual.

In most African societies witches would be first described as morose, unsociable people; people who eat alone so that they need not share their food, but who can be dangerous if others do not share food with them; arrogant people who pass by others without greeting them; people who are readily offended. A person who gazes fixedly at others is often thought to be a witch and be trying to convey an injury in the look; on the other hand, the Mandari of the southern Sudan, who associate most witches with the 'evil eye', say that persons who have it will not look you straight in the face. But their sly glances from eyes which 'go round and round' are just as dangerous. Some peoples distinguish possessors of the evil eye from witches proper, and regard their actions as less heinous. But witches are very often supposed to have red eyes, and one cannot but suppose that this emphasis on eyes and staring is associated with a general idea that staring can do harm.

Just as the night-witch epitomises all kinds of unthinkable evils, the everyday witch is the image of what one would not wish one's neighbours to be, and many unpopular people have the qualities ascribed to witches. Nobody in an African village goes about in terror of all his unsociable neighbours, but other things being equal – and it will be later shown that they seldom are – such a person might well be accused of a particular act of witchcraft. But it is a truism that unpopular persons are more likely to be suspected of anti-social actions than popular ones.

But a significant effect of this kind of witchcraft belief is that it keeps before all minds the idea of the kind of behaviour that should be avoided in relations with one's neighbours. In particular, children are warned against the kind of behaviour that may, if they persist in it, lead people to think they are witches. Also, since witches are thought to be quick to take offence, the danger of incurring their anger can be made an argument against any deviation from the accepted code of manners.

But, because theories of witchcraft must be made applicable to every situation where anyone seeks to invoke them, there is no reason why a witch should conform to the stereotype. Witches are very clever, and know what they are supposed to be like; so a witch may conceal his cantankerous nature under an assumed bonhomie. This will very likely be overdone so that the witch gives himself away. All the same, this rider to the general proposition once more widens the field within which suspicion is plausible. The Mandari of the southern Sudan say that witches are ugly as well as disagreeable, dirty and unkempt. But in the same breath they will tell you that witches are – and are not pretending to be – unusually attractive, and that this lures people into marrying them and so perpetuating their inheritance of evil. It is possible also to believe, as the Gisu of eastern Uganda do, that everyday witches are in no way distinguishable from ordinary people.

Another characteristic that is associated with witchcraft in egalitarian societies, such as those of small scale and simple technology often are, is one that the world of strenuous competition approves: hard work in the production of material goods. Where there is little scope for the acquisition of wealth, people seem to resent the small degree of superiority that is attainable at least as much as the poor resent riches in countries where the gap is wide. They believe that a good neighbour should not seek to outdistance his fellows. If someone does, it is *their* envy that ascribes this to something other than his own efforts, something discreditable –

perhaps he employs familiars to work on his land at night, or draws the fertility of other people's crops to his own garden.

Successful hunters may be credited with the same powers. In their case there is even more reason, since there are in hunting elements both of luck and of a kind of skill that is not easily taught; moreover, when they are away by themselves in the bush they may be communing with all kinds of sinister beings, or collecting medicines to be used in sorcery. The Ndembu, who believe that the unusually diligent farmer must have familiars to work for him during the night, also believe that a good hunter has his familiars, and that to secure their services he must kill a junior relative by sorcery; and the spirit who, they think, confers the gift of divination is also associated with hunting. The prophet Bwanali, who after the Second World War had a great reputation in Malawi and Zambia as a healer and protector against witchcraft, had been a hunter for much of his life. Hunters have this kind of reputation in West Africa too.

In New Guinea, where on the whole little responsibility for sickness or misfortune is placed on witches, there is one people, the Tangu on the north coast, who believe in a type of person roughly equivalent to them. He is called the *ranguma*. The first *ranguma*, they say, was the last man to appear when the ancestors of the Tangu came out of a hole in the earth (the manner in which many New Guinea peoples are believed to have come into being). 'He brought with him poison and [the means and ability to cause] sickness and death. He was arrogant and proud, and proclaimed that all things were his.'[10] He is thought of as a person who seeks to assert his superiority over others instead of being content with recognition as their equal.

The *ranguma* then in himself is the explanation of evil; he is human, but not just an ordinary human with special knowledge of sorcery such as so many New Guinea peoples believe in. He can be recognised by his disagreeable behaviour, his red eyes (though there are no evil-eye notions here), and 'the splay hand and long fingers of a strangler'. He is capable of material as well as mystical crimes; he may kill by direct violence as well as by sorcery. He does not do harm by hatred alone; on the contrary, he is believed to kill in cold blood. The Tangu do not believe in punitive spirits, but they do not hold the *ranguma* responsible for *all* sickness. Some may be the sufferer's fault; if he has wronged a neighbour the latter was entitled to put a spell on him. He must confess and make reparation. But if he then does not recover, it must be that the wronged neighbour who will not relent – or someone else – is a *ranguma*.

Persons in certain social categories are sometimes held to be particularly prone to witchcraft. Not surprisingly, these are people who in some sense or other are not full members of the community. A striking example is provided by the Mandari of the southern Sudan. In a Mandari chiefdom there is one landowning lineage which provides the chief, and a number of dependent or client lineages believed to be descended from outsiders who at one time or another sought refuge there. Although this relationship may date from a long-distant past, the foreign origin of the clients is not forgotten, and individuals among them are not only suspected of witchcraft but publicly accused, for example in the insulting songs sung by the young men at dances against the people of rival chiefdoms. One very obvious reason for such a theory is that it provides the landowning lineage with a good reason why they need not divide their own ranks by suspicions and accusations. Another is that the landowners are genuinely afraid that a dependent lineage whose numbers and wealth have increased may seize control of the chiefdom from them, as has sometimes happened. Another is that the clients, like all dependents, resent their dependence, and so may be reasonably thought to harbour hostility against their protectors.

Yet another, even among a people with so little obvious social differentiation, is the ascription to a lower class of qualities which are disapproved.

Persons of mixed descent may be considered open to suspicion – again because they are thought to be not fully integrated into the community and therefore lacking in that sense of goodwill towards their neighbours that its members ought to have; and the suspicion directed against them may be augmented by a belief, that is very general among people who believe in mystical powers, that those of foreigners are always more deadly.

Hereditary witches

Most African peoples believe that witchcraft 'runs in families', whether they suppose that it is an inherited quality or that parents teach it to their children. In the latter case it might well be argued that one could not teach it to a person who was born without the capacity for it, but a more likely reason for such a supposition is that, in societies where there is no wage labour, it is usually from their parents that people learn any craft.

There are different views about the direction from which the inheritance comes. The Zande, who believe that a person's sex depends on the question whether the father's or the mother's soul was stronger at the time of conception, logically suppose that a person who has witchcraft substance must have got this from the parent of the same sex. The same belief is held by the Gisu of Mount Elgon, though there it does not appear to rest on theories about the source of an individual's sex, and it can, like most witch-craft beliefs, be modified so that suspicions and accusations can be directed in accordance with the opinions of the supposed victim of witchcraft or his kin. For the Gisu, although in principle mystical powers are inherited from the parent of the same sex, it is possible for magic, good or evil, to be taught to a person by the other parent or his kin (it can also be given away or sold, though this is said to be rare).

Other peoples think witchcraft is inherited in accordance with the principle of descent recognised for the purposes of inheritance of property and succession to office – i.e. either through mothers or through fathers, but in the same line whatever the sex of the supposed witch. Others – for example, the Nyakyusa – think that a child of either sex may inherit witchcraft from either parent, but unless both are witches, the child need not necessarily become one. Some believe that witchcraft power, as well as other mystical powers, is transmitted by the parent other than the one from whom property is inherited. This is made very explicit among the Tallensi of northern Ghana, who believe that witchcraft powers are transmitted to persons of both sexes by their mothers, and make no bones about saying so. Fortes relates how a person presenting a uterine kinsman (for example, a son or daughter of his mother's sister) will explain the relationship by saying: 'If he can fly through the air, then I can; if he can see the future, then I can'.[11] As he remarks, such a matter-of-fact way of referring to the subject is only possible because the Tallensi do not often resort to accusations of witchcraft when they are in trouble.

What is interesting here is the question whether numbers of people are open to suspicion because they are thought to have witchcraft 'in the family', and how this affects their relationship with their neighbours. One will find it stated in connection with African marriage that parents will object to their children (particularly their sons) marrying into a lineage said to be tainted by witchcraft, but one does not read of whole descent-groups who cannot find marriage partners, or are obliged to look for them among people who carry the same stigma. Evans-Pritchard remarks of the Zande that a member of the ruling lineage is never accused of witchcraft by a commoner because that would amount to asserting that all the royal line were witches; but one can think of other reasons why it would be impolitic to make such an accusation.

But the belief in the inheritance of witchcraft may be appealed to in reverse, by Zande and by other peoples as well, when a person accused defends himself by the argument that no member of his lineage has ever been convicted of witchcraft. And where an autopsy has been performed and no witchcraft substance has been identified, this can be held to exonerate a whole lineage; indeed this was one of the purposes for which autopsies were made. Jean La Fontaine states of the Gisu that 'a person's close agnates are always implicated if he is accused of being a witch', but does not tell us how this affects them.

The Mandari idea that clients are disposed towards witchcraft because of their relationship to their landowning patrons is reinforced by the notion that witchcraft is hereditary – since client status is also hereditary – and it is on record there that when marriages are being planned people avoid lineages supposed to be tainted. Jean Buxton observed there that members of suspect lineages marry among themselves or with people who have a bad reputation for some other offence, such as theft. While she was living among the Mandari a man whose son was accused of witchcraft killed him rather than have the stigma of a 'bad' heredity enter his line of descendants; she also knew two sons – one legitimate, one bastard – of a man who was said to have been expelled from his village as a supected witch. Witchcraft had come to be associated with the lineages of both. Both were diviners and healers, hence professionally opposed to witches. But rumour ascribed mishaps to them, and a death was laid at the door of one, who was publicly lampooned in a hostile song by youths of another village. It is not easy to judge whether suspicion was directed at this man simply on account of his paternity.

The cases quoted do not demonstrate that the stigma is remembered through many generations, though it may be that it is. But it will be shown later that, whatever may be the ideology of witchcraft, suspicion usually rests on a person who has recently quarrelled with the supposed victim, and on somebody who is already unpopular.

An incident in Turner's long story of accusations and counteraccusations in an Ndembu village, which has been mentioned as one of our principal sources for the study of African witchcraft, illustrates the way in which theories about hereditary witchcraft can be modified to suit somebody's interests in a particular situation. In Mukanza village, where Turner did most of his work, there was intense rivalry between two related lineages. Turner's servant, Kasonda, who was a member of one of these, frequently told him that witchcraft through the activities of hereditary familiars was carried on by women of the other. One of these women, Ngamuwang'a, was in fact accused of having in this way caused the death of her husband, her sister and her sister's daughter. The sister had died in another village, and Kasonda had been sent there as representative of Mukanza to discuss the ritual payment which her death made necessary. In this discussion he sought to protect the honour of Mukanza village by saying that, contrary to universally held belief, the old woman had got her familiars from outside her lineage, from her mother-in-law. Certainly this was not usual; but in this case it had happened.

It is clear that the theory of the lineal inheritance of witchcraft is more likely to be found in societies where conflict arises between lineages who are neighbours, and that it is likely to be invoked when such a conflict exists. And when an actual death is in question, a woman closely related to one who has been accused before may well be an object of suspicion. But there is no question here of lineages which are publicly stigmatised or rejected in the planning of marriages. What Evans-Pritchard[12] says of the Zande seems to be widely true:

Azande generally regarded witchcraft as an individual trait and it is treated as such in spite of its association with kinship. At the same time certain clans . . . had a reputation for witchcraft in the reign of King Gbudwe . . . No one thinks any worse of a man if he is a member of one of these clans.

In fact, the association of a whole lineage with witchcraft is apt to be asserted only as part of an expression of general hostility between groups, as the examples already quoted show.

3 Protection against witches

People who consider that some hidden enemy may at any time attack them by mystical means may seek to protect themselves in advance – by individual precautions or by actions of different kinds taken on behalf of a whole community by those who are responsible for its welfare.

Of the peoples who have been well described, the Zande do most in the way of individual precautions. Their method is not unlike that of the Chinese, who consult a specialist to find out what day is most auspicious for an undertaking, or perhaps more like that of the Greeks and Romans, who would take omens when about to embark on an enterprise and put it off if the omens were not good.

Oracles

The Zande use methods which have come to be called oracles in the literature of anthropology, though an oracle used to be thought of as a voice which answered questions, and in this case the answer is not given in spoken words. Oracles of this kind are employed in the detection of witches as well as for the purpose of avoiding them.

The Zande seeking to know what course he had best pursue puts questions which are supposedly answered by the behaviour of some object. As long as the object of the consultation is not to fix the responsibility for a death, in which case the royal oracle must be consulted, he can do this for himself and make his own interpretation of what happens. The essence of the procedure is that the questions put can be answered by yes or no, so that the framing of them is a significant part of the process. They do not always refer directly to dangers of witchcraft. A man may ask, 'If I stay in my present house, shall I live long and prosper?'. By implication he is asking whether witchcraft threatens his life. The simplest method of all consists in sticking two branches into an ant-hill and looking next day to see which branch the ants have eaten. Then there is

Rubbing-board oracles are widely used in the Congo basin area. The Zande type are very simple and without decoration. This one from the Lele of the Kasai region is used in the same way, the knob being rubbed on the board while questions are asked.

what is called a 'rubbing-board'. This is an object made for the purpose; it consists of two little pieces of wood, one on legs so that it can stand on the ground and one which fits it like a cover. When questions are asked the upper board is rubbed against the lower, and the answer is given when it sticks. It is endowed with magical power by rubbing decoctions of roots into cuts made in the lower board, and it may be these cuts that sometimes prevent the upper one from moving smoothly, and thus give the supposed answer. Zande carry these little instruments about with them so that they can consult an oracle at any moment.

But the oracle on which they most rely is the behaviour of a chicken to which a poison, made from a wild creeper called *benge* and having some of the qualities of strychnine, has been administered. To be able to consult this oracle a man must have a supply of

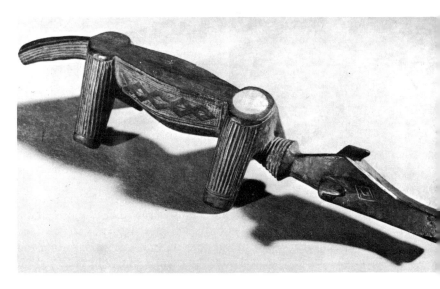

the poison and also a stock of chickens. Indeed Zande keep fowls primarily for this purpose rather than for food. The poison is made into a paste and forced into the chicken's beak. The answer to the enquirer's question depends on whether the chicken dies. The question, therefore, is put in the form, 'If so-and-so, *benge* kill the fowl,' and then its opposite, 'If so-and-so, *benge* spare the fowl'.

When an oracle is consulted about future events the implication of all questions, however they are framed, is to find whether a proposed journey, marriage, hunting expedition or whatever it may be, is threatened by witchcraft. If it is, it will be postponed or abandoned; hence an unfavourable oracle may sometimes provide an excuse for getting out of an inconvenient obligation, and people are said to offer this excuse even if it is not true. A man who is away from home may be advised by his rubbing-board oracle to leave his host's village secretly and at an unusual time, or to take a roundabout route so as to dodge the witchcraft that is lying in wait for him – a method of defence that is rather inconsistent with beliefs in its extraordinary powers. He can ask an oracle where it is safe for him to live or propitious for him to plant his crops, or who should perform the operation of circumcision on his son. A curious feature of Zande life is that some men consult an oracle regularly to know whether an enemy is threatening to make them ill by witchcraft, and if they are given such a warning, ask the oracle who is responsible and approach this person in just the same way as they would if they were already sick.

It will be noted that the traveller's method of dodging witchcraft is very simple, and would almost imply that it is something natural like a trap or an ambush laid in a fixed place. This idea might seem logically to presuppose other ideas, such as that the witch projects his witchcraft at a particular time and place, which are not recorded among Zande beliefs about the activities of witches. But, as Evans-Pritchard was the first to show, the corpus of witchcraft lore does not form a logical whole. Rather, it provides a range of ideas which can be invoked in different situations. A man who is looking for protection against future dangers will believe he can get the better of a witch if he takes the right precautions, while one who is already suffering will be more likely to dwell on those theories that ascribe almost invincible cunning to witches.

An unusual form of defence practised in parts of Zambia is associated with the belief which is widespread in western Zambia and Angola, that sorcerers have familiars. The familiar of an Ndembu man, called *ilomba*, is a water-snake with a human head – a replica of the sorcerer's own head. If the *ilomba* is shot, the sorcerer dies. But it cannot be shot by any ordinary weapon. The only one that can be used for this purpose is the 'night-gun', an object possessed by other sorcerers, who will use it for a fee. A night-gun is said to be made from a human thigh-bone, and primed with earth from a grave and pieces of the flesh of corpses. 'Shooting the *ilomba*' is not regarded as a justifiable act, but when someone who has been suspected of sorcery dies, it may be alleged that this is what killed him.

This is as unreal as most methods of fighting the unreality of witchcraft. But the 'night-guns' exist and may be seen in the Rhodes-Livingstone Museum. Moreover, in recent years, more powerful weapons, made of metal and firing such missiles as finger-bones as well as pieces of metal, have been used to commit real murders of suspected witches. But the gunmen, as those who were actually accused of murder have been called, did not, or did not all, suppose themselves to be engaged in straightforward physical killing. One said as he fired his weapon at his victim 'If you are a witch you must die tonight, but if you are not, you must not die'.[1] Although this kind of action may seem to resemble retribution rather than protection, I mention it here because it does not follow an accusation. The modern method may well be conceived by those who practise it as a form of self-help to which the victims of witchcraft are driven because the courts will no longer listen to their accusations. It should be noted that the mystical element is present in the belief that the person shot at will not be injured unless he is actually guilty.

In the Akan-speaking parts of Ghana people go for individual protection to one or other of the shrines of new deities who, it is said, have made their existence known in recent years. They manifest themselves by possessing men who thereafter act as their priests and mediums, and who are thought to be more powerful than the gods of ancient tradition. These deities are thought to demand the services of some individual as priest and medium, and to show their wish by driving him mad. A person so 'possessed' runs wild in the bush, and it is the responsibility of those who already are able to make contact with mystical beings to identify the spirit responsible and build a temple to him. To these temples come people who think they are victims of witchcraft, people who believe they are themselves witches, and people seeking protection. These last promise to repay a year's freedom from ills ascribed to witchcraft by making an offering to the spirit. A person who has done this forfeits the spirit's protection if he steals, commits adultery or himself is guilty of witchcraft or sorcery. If, after making his pact with the spirit, he is guilty of any of these offences, it will kill him or drive him mad; but as long as he keeps to the elementary rules of good conduct it will punish those who attack him by mystical means. The supplication made here is not for general prosperity but specifically for protection against witchcraft – an indication that it looms as large in Akan as in Zande cosmology.[2]

It would take too long to catalogue the multitude of amulets and charms that individuals in every society wear or keep in their houses as defence against witches. The study of these belongs to the field of symbolism rather than of conduct, since a person who supposes he has been attacked by witchcraft does not consider the inadequacy of his charms as a reason.

The mystical fight against witches

Many peoples regard it as part of the duty of the persons in authority to protect the community against the attacks of witches. The best known of these are the Nyakyusa, whose beliefs about witches have been mentioned. A chief or village headman is thought of as 'watching over the country by day and by night', and the night watch, which is also sometimes described as 'war by night', is the war against witches. The power that witches are thought to derive from the python in their entrails is somehow associated with pythons in general, so chiefs and headman must have them also,

This Kongo figure has not been pierced with nails in order to cause someone's death by sorcery. It is the image of a spirit; piercing it with a nail is believed to release the spirit's power for the benefit of the person seeking its aid.

and an important part of the ritual that they go through before entering on their office is the drinking of medicines which give them the power of seeing and fighting witches. Most accession rites include some kind of magical treatment of the new chief which is believed to give him a mystical source of power, but it is unusual to find such explicit reference to defence against witches. The medicine a chief is given to drink is the most powerful of all, so powerful that only he and not the headmen who are his subordinates may use it. It is said to be made from the flesh of an enormous python, and to have the very power that a witch has, of mystical killing. People other than chiefs, it is thought, sometimes get hold of it and use it to make themselves important beyond their station. But what the Nyakyusa fear most is that if this medicine gets out of control it will actually perform witchcraft – that is, kill men and cattle and eventually its owner. Here one has a theory of witchcraft which does not ascribe it to human malevolence activating a mystical power, but to the power itself. A case in the chief's court was recorded by Monica Wilson.[3] The chief asked: 'Why does this thing go about at night? I have seen it myself, it shines, I know it. It is that with which the doctors treat us chiefs . . . It kills you people'. The man held to be causing the trouble was suspect because he was richer than his fellows, but he was accused, not of bewitching them, but of the illicit possession of a medicine which in authorised hands was a means of destroying witches. As Monica Wilson puts it, 'The shades [spirits of the dead], medicines and witchcraft are distinguished and are thought to operate independently, but they are all manifestations of a mystical power which is logically one, though none of our informants saw it as that.'[4]

The Nyakyusa imagine that every night a battle is fought between good and bad pythons, in which the defenders use spears and may kill a witch-python, with the result that its human owner dies. The defenders are also believed to see the human witches in dreams.

This power is given to the headman by the medicines which he drinks, but other people can have it too; indeed, the experience of dreaming that somebody is a witch proves to the person who has it that he has the defensive power. It is almost surprising that everyone does not claim to have it. A defender who has thus recognised a witch should make his identity known. The defence is not impregnable – obviously, since cases of witchcraft occur. Witches are more persistent than defenders; they attack every night, whereas defenders may take a night off. Moreover, since the coming of European government, accusations have not been officially countenanced, and this, it is believed, encourages the activity of the witches.

The Tiv of central Nigeria hold a somewhat similar belief, namely, that the power which is effective in witchcraft is one that can also produce socially approved results. Paul and Laura Bohannan[5] say that the widest meaning of the word *tsav*, which describes this power, is simply 'ability'; it is any quality in which a man excels his neighbours. All markedly fortunate people are thought to have *tsav*, just as elsewhere they may be suspected of sorcery. Possessors of *tsav* (*mbatsav*) have the power of remedying the ills of the community by performing the appropriate ritual; this, it is thought, in some cases necessitates the sacrifice of a human being, which is believed to be, and may have once been, performed secretly at night. It is the elders who have this power and this responsibility, but it may be that they sometimes use their power simply so as to enjoy a cannibal feast. They may also refrain from using it on behalf of a particular person. But it is so much taken for granted that it is their duty to protect the community from harm that when a death is ascribed to witchcraft they are asked 'Why have you not prevented it?'

All peoples perform regular rituals – what are known as 'confirmatory' rites – in which they appeal for the blessing and protection of their ancestors or other spirits in the form of fertility of

This mask, from the Sankuru river area, represents a spiritual being who is invoked in the periodical witch-finding drives of the Songe. The bundle on the head probably contains objects representative of Songe cosmological ideas.

crops, cattle and people, and freedom from sickness. Occasionally the prayers spoken during such ceremonies refer expressly to protection against witches, but this has not often been recorded. However, it would follow from the interpretation of witchcraft that I am suggesting that the absence of prosperity is almost to be equated with the presence of witchcraft.

Two ceremonies may be cited in which witchcraft is explicitly mentioned. One is that held for the installation of the king (*Mukama*) of Bunyoro in western Uganda. As with the Nyakyusa chiefs and headmen the aim of this ritual is to endow the chief by mystical means with the qualities that he needs to make him a successful ruler. He is not himself to be a defender of his people against witches (or sorcerers, for Bunyoro is one of the places where they are not distinguished); this function falls to others. But there is a point at which the participants express their defiance of enemies, and so confidence in their ability to resist them, in the phrase 'You enemies, you witches, you barbarians, why are you disobeying this our brave Mukama?' The phrase is from an account of the accession rites written in English by a recent Mukama.[6]

The Nyakyusa used to perform at the new year – the beginning of the rainy season – a ceremony which was called 'throwing out the rubbish'. The essence of this was that all fires were let to go out, the ashes thrown away and new fires lit. Many reasons were given for the clearing out of the ashes; not only witches but the shades of the ancestors were thought to have contaminated the hearth. The shades, it was said, 'bring sickness' when they come to warm themselves at the fire in the homestead, while the danger from witches was that they might have roasted the flesh of their victim over his own fire. The annual ceremony was no longer being performed when the Wilsons worked in Nyakyusa country, but it was still held when there was some public affliction or an evil omen. While they were there it was done to cure a plague of rats in one part of the country,

in another on account of what may have been an epidemic of typhoid. In the latter case people's fears were exacerbated by what they considered an unheard-of event – a ground hornbill ate a fowl in one of the villages. Old men commenting on the significance of the ritual used the phrases 'The filth which the witches and the shades have brought to us', and 'The witches and shades gather and bring sickness together'.[7] The difference between the activity of the shades and that of the witches is that the shades are within their rights, the witches not; nevertheless, the Nyakyusa, like some other African peoples, fear the objects of their religion, and their rituals are more concerned with keeping them at a distance than with bringing them closer. When they come close it is important that they should come in benevolent mood. In addition to the scattering of the ashes this rite of purification includes the shouting by women of a war cry against the angry shade, who is being driven away so that he may come back without the anger that caused the sickness (or may have caused it, if witches did not). This linking of shades and witches, as if they acted together, is one of many examples of the difficulty of distinguishing between the forces of good and evil.

Other peoples have regular throwing-out rituals which are not

The Master (in 1936) of the order
of doctor-diviners in Nupe
with his store of medicines.

65

specifically directed against witches, but are conceived as ridding a community of evil in general or sickness in particular. An example very recently recorded is the 'taking out of *yamo*' by the Padhola of eastern Uganda, when a spirit held to be responsible for much sickness is symbolically removed from one part of the country to another and finally right out of its borders.[8]

Rituals to expel witches

Some peoples, however, have regular rituals the specific purpose of which is to rid the country of witches. Of these the one that has been most fully described is that of the Nupe in northern Nigeria. All such performances have been frowned on by colonial rulers, who have held that, since witchcraft is not real, accusations of witchcraft must be false and punishment for it must be unjust. They have further held that to claim magical powers is fraudulent and that people can be justly punished for making such claims. This has made it possible for their subjects in some places to bring cases in the courts of chiefs against persons making – or alleged to make – claims which the government holds to be false while the accuser believes them to be true. But attempts to detect secret practitioners who have made no claims cannot so easily be brought within the four corners of the law.

Nevertheless, the Nupe ceremony was being performed up to 1922, and so was well remembered when Nadel was in the Nupe kingdom ten years later.[9] It was performed by members of a secret society known as *ndakó gboyá*, who claimed to have special control of a mysterious mystical force, into the knowledge of which they were initiated by the descendant of a famous detector of witches. This man does not belong to mythical times but to the nineteenth century; it was only after 1860 that the owner of the secret began to teach it to others and so to build up a society with 'lodges' in different villages. This is worth remembering in view of the fact that the witch-finding movements of which there have been so many in the present century are commonly interpreted as reactions against colonial laws prohibiting traditional methods of dealing with witches.

The society might perform its ritual for the general benefit of the village in which a 'lodge' was situated, or might be called on to lend its aid at the sacrifice for prosperity which used to be performed every year, and to be the most important Nupe ceremony. Its contribution consisted in a dance of one or more persons disguised in a peculiar kind of mask, not a representation of a grotesque head like most West African masks, but a cylinder of white cloth which completely covered the dancer. Inside it was a pole fastened to a wicker frame on top, by means of which the mysterious white figure could be made to bend and swoop. The spirit within the mask was supposed to have the mystical power of detecting evil of any kind. When Nadel was in Nupe country in 1934–6 the society had not been fully suppressed, although it had had to give up its witch-finding activities, and he was able to see the *ndakó gboyá* dance.

The *ndakó gboyá* would be invited to a village which, in Nadel's phrase, felt itself threatened by witches (who, in this society, are always believed to be women). He does not indicate whether this implies that disaster had already struck and the dance was intended to detect the guilty; but since most people who believe in witchcraft think they are threatened at all times, this might not be a necessary condition. Moreover, at the end of the performance that Nadel witnessed, although there was no question of marking down women as witches, people were saying that the village was now free from them, and it seems that the contribution of the masked dancers to other rituals is held to consist essentially in frightening witches away by the possession of a mystical power even stronger than theirs.

The *ndakó-gboyá* mask.

The performance is intended to be, and on that occasion was, awe-inspiring. Nobody knew the identity of the dancer in the mask, and nobody but the village authorities knew there was to be a performance. There were two masked dancers, never seen together; one appeared unheralded at dawn, and when he disappeared in one direction the second would appear from another quarter. As a spectator put it 'They spring from the ground and are swallowed by the ground'. The songs sung by the crowd welcomed them with reservations – looking forward to their departure and calling on the protection of God against them. The protector here is as alarming as that against which he protects; it is one of the few contexts in which the cliché, 'the dreaded witch-doctor', bears some relation to reality.

When the witch-finding performances were allowed, the women of the village that was being cleansed were gathered in the market-place, and the masked figure would swoop on one and another in turn. The accused woman was taken into the bush and made to scratch the ground with her finger-nails; if blood came she was a witch. Some of Nadel's informants said that a witch thus proved guilty was killed at once, but others denied this. In any case she could buy herself off by a payment.

Shortly before the society was suppressed it had taken to organising witch-finding tours, visiting places that had not sought its services, and demanding money to go away as well as the ransom paid by suspected witches. According to the leader of the society, whom Nadel knew, in the years just after 1918 the whole country was seized by a fear of witchcraft. But if this was indeed so, the remedy proved worse than the disease. People who had nothing left to pay their taxes complained to the government, and these activities were banned.

R. S. Rattray, the first ethnographer to work in Ashanti in Ghana, described in less detail a dance against witches that he actually witnessed.[10] The performers in this case were women, attendants on the shrine of a 'fetish' known as Fwemso, the cult of which was suppressed at about the same time that the *ndakó gboyá* was declared illegal in Nigeria. By a fetish is meant an object which is believed to have mystical powers but not to be the abode of a personalised being. As Rattray remarks, the cult of Fwemso had as much elaboration as that of the many minor deities who are worshipped in Ashanti. It had a temple on the shore of Lake Bosomtwe, the extraordinary circular lake near Kumasi which is believed to be the home of one of the principal Ashanti deities. Rattray visited the temple and made a drawing of the shrine, which was too dark for a satisfactory photograph. Its central feature consisted of life-size models in clay of a pair of female breasts, set on a column covered in cloth, and adorned with a garland of leaves. Above this stood a little wooden figure, masculine in appearance, which represented Fwemso, and there were five other such figures, three male and two female. The symbolism of these objects would be for a later interpreter to unravel if this is still possible.

The aim of the dance here was not to detect and denounce individuals. It was believed rather that it lured the witches to destruction by activating the fetishes (the little figures) to appear like witches and make the call by which they summon one another. When the witches appeared, they would be caught and killed. The song that accompanied the dance included the words 'Someone is going to die'. But its supposed effect was that the witches would save their lives by voluntary confession and repentance, and by handing over the 'pot of witchcraft' which they were believed to use. Rattray states that Fwemso, when it was suppressed, 'was being used for purposes of blackmail and extortion', but does not tell us anything more specific.

In recent years the temples of minor gods have become places of resort for persons troubled by witchcraft or seeking protection from it, but in Rattray's time, just after the First World War, it was held that they could not be consulted because they were themselves afraid of the witches. An old witchfinder whom Rattray knew claimed that when he was engaged in his profession the priests of the gods would regard him as their superior.

As the performances of the *ndakó gboyá* are described by Nadel their seems to be little opportunity for the masked dancer to be briefed in advance as to the preferred suspects; particularly as the identity of the dancer is kept a close secret, so that he could hardly be approached beforehand, even if the dance was being held in his home village. On the other hand, since, although there are slits in the mask which supposedly represent his eyes, he cannot really see where he is going, he has to be guided by two attendants; and it may well be that they choose their victims in response to the reaction of the onlookers. This would bring this performance into the category of means of assigning responsibility for alleged acts of witchcraft.

The same might be said of the Zulu 'smelling out' of witches. This phrase has gained wide currency simply because of the long period of time that people in Europe have had to pick up ideas about customs in South Africa. In fact the idea that evil has a smell which appropriately endowed persons can recognise is not very common, in Africa or elsewhere.

The most dramatic account of a 'smelling-out' is given in Ritter's *Shaka Zulu*, a fictionalised biography by a South African who collected Zulu traditions of their famous king from old men of the royal lineage. The occasion of this, as preserved in their memories, was the appearance of a series of evil omens resembling those which led Nyakyusa chiefs to order a 'cleansing of the country'. A porcupine came into the royal village; two cows were killed by lightning; and a crow was said to have spoken in human language. A woman diviner was called in, and ordered a 'smelling-out' in which she took the principal part. This was introduced by a dance in which five witch-finders worked themselves up into the appropriate psychological condition, but this dance was not here part of the detection process. The latter consisted in a proclamation by the witch-finders declaring that they could smell the thoughts and designs of the evil-minded, after which they ordered the assembled population to sing so that the witch-finders could smell their breath. This was followed by a new dance in which they imitated dogs pursuing a scent, and when it had been going on for some time they began to identify the guilty. As Ritter describes the scene, the chanting would become louder as they approached a man who was the object of general suspicion or unpopularity, whereas it was hushed when a popular man seemed to be in danger, so that in fact the accusations made would be in accordance with public opinion.

There is inevitably a good deal of recreative imagination in this description, but anthropologists would not regard it as improbable. Ritters' informants may have been sceptical about the mystical powers of the witch-finders, as we learn from a later passage in his book that Shaka himself was, and have guessed that they were guided by the reaction of the crowd. Less sceptical people might have said that, if it seemed that a generally popular man was to be revealed as a witch, people were too shocked or awe-struck to keep up the volume of their singing. Some might have interpreted the increase in sound when an unpopular man was to be marked down as an expression of approval *after* the identification had been made.

But the principle is clear, and it can be applied to every public procedure of witch-detection. If the verdicts of the smellers-out, or of any other detectors of witches, were not in line with general expectations, their methods would not command public confidence. Despite the theory that their mystical powers give them knowledge denied to the common run of men, they are not implicitly trusted. The possibility of a wrong decision is by no means excluded, though this is more likely to be ascribed to the action of witchcraft in confusing the issue than to the inadequacy of the practitioner.

A less dramatic and less alarming ritual is that performed by the Arusha, who live on the slopes of Mount Meru in Tanzania.[11] This does not recur at a fixed time, but is performed when there is a feeling of unease, often because women are having reproductive difficulties. In this case it is the women who perform the ritual, but suspicion of witchcraft is not confined to them. All the women in a body enter each homestead in turn and dance singing round every house in it. A woman who refused to take part, or a man who refused to allow his house to be cleansed in this way, would be suspected of witchcraft, but there is no question of applying tests to individuals. When P.H.Gulliver was there (in 1957) a Christian convert sought to demonstrate his repudiation of pagan beliefs by refusing to let the women dance round his house, but he had to give way in the end.

I conclude this chapter by referring to the ritual of protection of a very different part of the world – Bali in Indonesia. Bali is famed for the beauty and elaboration of its dance-rituals; their existence must be known to a far greater number of people than have any idea of their significance. All the dances are sacred, and enact stories which have religious significance for performers and spectators. Some of the most important portray the unmasking of witches and the vanquishing of their power of evil magic. To the Balinese the source of this evil power is a woman, a mythical widow, Rangda, who is believed to devour children. Rangda is the word for widow, and widowhood to the Balinese is a monstrous condition, since a good wife should follow her husband to the underworld, and, if she does not do so, remains in this one as the wife of a spirit. Among the dance-dramas that have been described by Beryl de Zoete,[12] one is concerned with the defeat of Rangda by a monster, Barong, who defends the Balinese against her. The other, Tjalonarang, tells a more elaborate story, in which a human witch and her disciples, and a witch-finder, all play parts. The latter drama is performed not only on ritually significant days but also when a village is afflicted by sickness. It has a number of local versions, but in essence it is concerned with the destruction of a witch. An interesting feature of this story is that the witch is supposed to have become so without her own volition. Finding herself to be a witch, however, she delights in destruction and teaches her wicked arts to others. She is detected, in some versions, by a holy man, in others by a witch-finder in a trance, but at the moment when she is threatened with execution she turns into Rangda herself and almost destroys her accuser. The monster Barong appears and fights her.

English-speaking students of Balinese dance-drama have given

Rangda, as a widow, is thought to have evil powers because a virtuous widow should not survive her husband. Like many witches, she is believed to use these powers to cause the death of young children.

The monstrous figure of
the witch Rangda from the
Tjalonarang dance in Bali.

two versions of this performance. According to Beryl de Zoete, the witch is vanquished, but her death is not shown because of the fear that if it were, her servants the human witches might exact vengeance; but the dance is a challenge to her supremacy, a reminder that there is something to hold the balance against her and her servants. According to Miguel Covarrubias, in contrast, its purpose is to propitiate Rangda by commemorating her triumphs.[13]

One cannot draw a sharp line between the kind of ritual that is intended to challenge, frighten or mystically destroy any witches who may be about and the kind that is organised to deal with specific troubles or fears. Some of those just described are performed in case of actual distress caused by drought or widespread sickness. The dance of the Zande witch-doctors described by Evans-Pritchard, though it purports to answer the problems of particular individuals or warn them of dangers threatening them, is also, as he puts it, 'a fight against the powers of evil, a parade against witchcraft'.[14] It is intended to alarm any witches who may be present, and according to Zande belief there are always many.

4 The detection of witches

Since witchcraft is by definition an activity that cannot be detected by everyday means, it must be tracked down by the actions of people, or the manipulation of objects, believed to have mystical power to reveal secrets. The general term for processes of this kind is divination, 'the endeavour to obtain information about things future, or otherwise removed from ordinary perception, by consulting informants other than human'.[1] They can be divided into three main classes. Objects such as the Zande rubbing-board, which answer questions automatically, are usually referred to as oracles. In anthropological literature the word divination is commonly used for more complicated objects, the behaviour of which has to be interpreted by an expert who manipulates them. Both these processes have been called 'mechanical divination'. In the third type, hidden knowledge is revealed by men or women believed to have special powers, speaking as the mediums of spirits or otherwise in a condition of heightened excitement. Some diviners, though not all, are believed to have been called to their vocation by a supernatural experience. Most mediums are persons believed to have been summoned to the service of the spirit on whose behalf they speak by some kind of psychological disturbance. But it is possible to become a 'witch-doctor' simply by receiving appropriate instruction and ritual treatment from already qualified practitioners. This is the method recognised by the Zande.

'Witch-doctors'

Rattray, writing of the professional witch-finder in Ashanti,[2] remarked that the word used to describe him could be almost exactly translated 'witch-doctor'; and it is true that the old witch-doctor who was Rattray's friend said he detected witches when he was possessed by the monster Sasabonsam, who is believed to be in league with the witches and the enemy of the priests of the beneficient spirits. His title, Bonsam Komfo, in fact means 'priest' of witches, and is yet another illustration of the haunting belief that those who combat evil must do so through knowledge of it, and so may themselves be practitioners of it. In spite of this belief, which is freely expressed in most African societies, it is a serious error to suppose that the man called by this name is a person who holds his neighbours in awe and from whom they ought to be rescued by the enlightenment of true religion or of science. The cliché 'the dreaded witch-doctor' is most misleading, and the fact that its noun and adjective have become so nearly inseparable is a good reason why it would be better to give up using the noun.

Mary Kingsley,[3] though she used the word 'witch-doctor' in writing of her experiences on the West African coast in the 1890's, explained that it should really be expanded to 'combatant of the evils worked by witches and devils on human souls and human property'. The missionary writer A. T. Bryant, who in forty-five years from 1883 gained an unrivalled knowledge of Zulu folklore, has pointed out that, although the Zulu use the same word for a person who professes to cure sickness by physical means and one who claims to detect and counter the activities of witches, they distinguish between the two by qualifying the noun that describes both.[4] A doctor, as popularly conceived in Africa and elsewhere, is a person on whom you rely in difficulties, and in Africa one of your difficulties may be that you are bewitched. A witch is a person whose activities may be dreaded and from whom – if he had been identified – one would be chary of seeking help. The compound word definitely does not refer to a person whose characteristics are primarily those of a witch.

The Zande witch-doctor, like his Zulu counterpart, is physician, magician, and diviner, and the word that describes his mystical activities cannot be used of his everyday medical ones. He must be taught his profession by a qualified practitioner and must undergo a ritual of initiation; fathers may teach their sons, but anyone may learn the secrets of the craft for a fee. These consist in knowledge of the properties of plants, particularly those which are held to give the power of divining, and of the tricks by which the doctors purport to remove alien substances from the bodies of their patients. But a part of the training of a witch-doctor consists in actually eating a sufficient quantity of the divining medicines. These are said to give the diviner *mangu*, the same word that is used for the witchcraft substance that he purports to detect in others. There is a close parallel here with the defensive pythons that the Nyakyusa headman acquires by drinking magical potions and employs to combat the pythons of witches. But some practitioners prefer to use a different word, one which refers only to the medicines that give the divining power, and others say that if any diviner is actually a witch, this is because he happens to have been born with witchcraft substance before he ate anti-witchcraft medicine.

Zande divination is a public event, indeed the most interesting event of village life. A séance is held at the house of some man who has a problem troubling him, and it may be combined with the initiation of a new recruit to the profession. All doctors who are within convenient distance attend, perhaps half a dozen; it was said, in about 1930, that their numbers were increasing too fast and that their skill was decreasing in proportion. Any person present may put a question to any one of them. The occasion is one of great excitement, generated by drumming and singing. The diviners dance, shaking hand-bells and making a clatter with wooden bells round their waists and bunches of rattling seeds round their arms and legs. After a concerted opening performance, individuals dance in reply to questions put to them. The dancing is supposed to activate the medicines which give the answer to the man who has eaten them; he dances until he is breathless and exhausted, then recovers himself and speaks. As Evans-Pritchard remarks,[5] while he may be thinking what to answer all the time he is dancing, this is clearly not a matter purely of detached reasoning. What the practitioners themselves interpret as the activity of the medicines they have eaten that morning is the effect of the general rhythmic noise and exhausting movement; as they describe what happens, the medicines suddenly make the diviner's heart beat faster at the thought of a particular name, and this is the name of the witch. But he does not openly denounce the witch; he speaks in hints which will mean more to the man consulting him than to the rest of the audience, and leaves his client to draw his own conclusions. As Evans-Pritchard reminds us, he believes in the dangers of witch-craft as firmly as any of his clients, and he does not wish to expose himself to the revenge of somebody he has accused, which could be directed against him at a time when he was not protected by his anti-witchcraft medicines. He is an everyday member of the com-munity, not a specialist called in from outside who does not have to live with the consequences of his diagnosis.

Evans-Pritchard's study of the witch-doctor's place in Zande society is the best possible corrective to the notion of the 'dreaded witch-doctor'. In Zande eyes he is not the only, or the most reliable, detector of witches; a man who has consulted a witch-doctor checks his answers by reference to one of the oracles which are believed to be more reliable because they operate automatically. But he is 'a special agent summoned from time to time with a general commission to ferret out witch-activities in the neighbour-hood and to protect people against them'.[6] In the heightened atmosphere of a séance he is an impressive and perhaps even alarm-ing figure, particularly in view of the Zande theory of witchcraft as something innate of which its possessor may not even be aware. Anyone at a séance may find that he is denounced as a witch, and although names are rarely named, in Evans-Pritchard's view people are always afraid that they will be. Moreover, he was present on one occasion where this did happen; the accused person, however, was not struck with terror but got up and threatened to knife the diviner, who then danced again and gave a different answer – and later said in private that the accused man's behaviour was an admission of guilt.

But in everday life he has as much prestige, and no more, than that enjoyed in Europe by a consultant physician outside his hospital. He has special knowledge which others lack, but these others are well aware of the jealousies and quarrels between different specialists, and regard them with amusement. A witch-doctor of high repute is consulted by the princes and nobles who command the greatest respect in Zande society, and this gives him a certain prestige; but it is the prestige of a favoured employee, like that of some musicians in the eighteenth century. But those who do not attain eminence in their profession are objects neither of admiration nor of dread, and indeed are often said to be charlatans, though there is no Zande who rejects entirely the belief in the witch-doctor's powers, and there cannot be as long as all Zande are convinced of the reality of witchcraft. Moreover, they do not spend all their time practising their profession; most of the time they are farming their fields or hunting in the bush like their neighbours.

It is a peculiarity of the Zande witch-doctors that they claim to derive their power of divination solely from the medicines they eat, and thus to speak in their own name and not in that of some spirit which is making them its mouthpiece. The Zande are unusual in assuming that witchcraft is responsible for all their troubles, and not considering the just anger of some spiritual being as a possible alternative. More commonly diviners who do not rely on mechanical means are believed to speak in the name of some spirit by which they are possessed, and this spirit is expected to identify one among various possible sources of the trouble about which the diviner is consulted.

A Nyoro diviner sitting outside his house to pose for his photograph. He divines when possessed by a spirit: the bowl in front of him is for offerings to the spirit. He would not actually practise his profession out of doors.

Spirit mediums

The Nyoro, in the west of Uganda, consult men who they believe are possessed by spirits (called *mbandwa*) and reveal secret matters as their mouthpieces.[7] Nyoro traditional religion was built around such spirits. They bore the names of ancient kings of a mythical dynasty that is supposed to have founded the kingdom and then mysteriously disappeared. Different lineages were under the guardianship of different spirits, and each had a medium through which the *mbandwa* could communicate with the living by 'mounting into his (or her) head'. In recent years great numbers of new *mbandwa* have appeared, just as the minor spirits are said to have multiplied in Ghana. The new *mbandwa*, who are distinguished from the old by being called 'black', are not the guardian spirits of particular lineages; their mediums are persons much more like the Zande witch-doctors, who will identify the source of mystical sickness for a fee. Beattie holds, as do many of those who have studied contemporary ways of detecting witchcraft and sorcery in Africa, that this increase is a response to the increase of anxiety among African populations which find themselves disoriented by the changes that have been thrust on them, first by colonial rule and mission teaching, and now by their own westernised rulers. It would be difficult to measure or compare the quantity of anxiety in African societies at different times, but an indisputable fact is that today very many Africans earn cash incomes and can pay to consult spirit mediums. Indeed, Beattie offers this also as an explanation of the proliferation of new *mbandwa*. A large number of the questions put to these mediums are aimed at identifying sorcerers. Nyoro believe that the new 'black' *mbandwa* themselves practise sorcery, both by sending their tutelary spirits to afflict others, and by hiring out their knowledge to kill the enemies of people who consult them. The remedy for affliction by a *mbandwa* is to become a member of his cult, and to be initiated into the cult a person must pay a fee to the medium who organises the initiation; this is a field in which the opportunities for exploitation are clear.

It is obvious that there is more room for flexibility in this kind of divination than there is where the behaviour of an inanimate object is held to give a yes-or-no answer. Intermediate between these methods is that in which the diviner interprets the behaviour of an inanimate object. But it is essential to any of these processes that the possible answers are limited by the ideas that present themselves to the consultant. The medium may be expected to guess what is troubling his client; but he guesses within a recognised range of likely troubles, and the answer he gives may be far from explicit. If he diagnoses witchcraft as the cause he may still stop short of identifying the witch. Thus a Tswana diviner might say, 'The wife of an older brother has bewitched you', or 'Your trouble comes from the righteous anger of an older kinsman,'[8] and a Ghanaian medium may simply advise someone to move out of reach of a witch who is harming him.

Oracle operators

A person who is in trouble or concerned about the possibility of trouble in the future may either operate an oracle for himself, as has been described in the case of the Zande, or consult a specialist. Privately-operated oracles must work on yes-or-no principles, since the ability to read the meaning of a combination of symbols calls for special knowledge. The Zande rubbing-board and termite oracles (see page 53) give straightforward answers to simple questions, but when poison is administered to chickens the most elaborate care is taken to check the results. A question is put twice over (two chickens are used), and unless the same answer is given at each test the oracle is held to be inconclusive. Then the same question is put in negative form.

The Zande do not conceive this as a simple mechanical test, but believe that the poison is in some mysterious way considering the problem while it is in the body of the chicken. Hence they do not administer it to fully-grown birds because, they say, such birds die too quickly, before the poison has had a chance to consider its answer. The administration of the poison and the questioning of the oracle – that is the poison, making its answer known by the reaction of the chicken – are held to call for considerable skill, and there may be three persons present at a consultation, whom Evans-

Pritchard calls the consultant, the operator and the questioner. The consultant is the man who wants to know the answer, and who provides the poison and the chickens, the operator the one who makes the chicken swallow the poison, and the questioner addresses the poison, often at some length, say for five or ten minutes at a time. One man may play all three roles, but most prefer to rely on friends whose skill they respect. But the skill is not that of a closed profession; it is a matter of intelligence and practice. The operator needs to know how much poison to give, how to jerk the chicken about to 'stir up the poison', and when it is time to throw it on the ground and see whether it dies or lives. The questioner must know how to put the questions so that the oracle understands them clearly, since, although it is addressed at such length, the actual matter it is called on to decide must be capable of a clear positive or negative answer. If several people take part in a consultation they agree on the question before it starts. This does not always take so crude a form as 'Is X responsible for my sickness?' Rather the oracle might be asked 'Does the sickness come from my own homestead or that of my wife's parents?' When the answer is received the consultant might either ask a more specific question, or go to the homestead held responsible and entreat its members as a body to withdraw the anger to which the sickness was ascribed.

As can be seen from this account, an oracle does not necessarily give an unambiguous answer, even when the method of consulting it seems designed to secure one. In this case, since the consultant frames the questions, it would seem that he may prefer to avoid naming possible enemies. When it is for a diviner to give the answer he may avoid the final conclusion in much the same way by saying 'The sickness comes from your father's brothers' or some other category of relatives.

Consultation of a supposedly automatic oracle whose answers nevertheless need interpretation is on the border of professional divination, in which the operator rather than the objects he manipulates is expected to give the answer the consultant is seeking. But not many processes of private divination are as elaborate as the consultation of *benge*. A number have been described from the Lugbara. The most widely used is the rubbing-stick, which operates on the same principle as the Zande rubbing-board. A twist of grass is rubbed up and down against a piece of cane while names are 'placed before it' – the names of persons, living or dead, who may be responsible for the trouble about which the oracle is consulted; obviously the operator himself chooses the names. The right name is indicated when the grass sticks. Another way of operating the rubbing-stick, used by the Nyoro, is for the operator to wet the stick and simply run his finger and thumb up and down it.

Lugbara use other oracles to confirm the answer given by the rubbing-stick, since neither it nor any other is assumed to be infallible. Or rather it is assumed that an oracle may be dishonest. People do not say that oracles make mistakes but that they 'tell lies', and that the chances that an answer from the rubbing-stick may be true or false are about equal. But it is always the oracle, and not the operator, that is supposed to be dishonest. The further oracles need not be operated by the same man whose rubbing-stick gave the first answer. They are all held to work independently of human manipulation and therefore to be more reliable.

The owner of a rubbing-stick oracle which has a reputation for 'telling lies' is held to be shamed by its behaviour rather than to be himself to blame. But he has to interpret what his oracle has 'said', and here there is room for differences in skill between one operator and another. The skill is held to be given by God, who conveys to a man in a dream that he has it. Only older men practise as rubbing-stick operators. Elders of lineages – the only holders of authority in Lugbara – often have their own rubbing-stick, but an elder does not become a professional operator of oracles. Such men are very often the younger brothers of elders. A man in that position cannot hope to attain independent authority, since an elder must be succeeded by his son, but he can gain influence and reputation as an oracle operator. Others with this skill are men who are feared as suspected witches. The confirmatory oracles may be operated by anyone who owns them; they do not require a supernatural authorisation.[9]

Diviners

A different method is employed by the Yombe of the Zambia-Malawi border. They, like many other peoples, regard it as a necessary part of mortuary ritual to discover by divination who is responsible for the death. To do so they send a man to hunt a duiker (a small antelope), and see whether he kills a male or a female. If the former, the death comes from the man's own kin, if the latter from his wife's. The questioning is repeated, each time offering two alternatives. This is a long-drawn-out process, involving a series of expeditions in pursuit of animals that are nowadays very scarce, and it may be given up before a clear answer is reached. This is particularly likely to happen if the answers point towards the people responsible for making the enquiry.[10]

We may describe as a diviner someone who does not purport to be speaking with the voice of a spirit, but who goes beyond the simple oracle operator in that he interprets the answer that is supposed to be given by the behaviour of the mechanical objects he uses. Oracle operators no doubt do this to some extent, but the essence of divination in this sense is that the process used allows for much greater complexity of interpretation. A very common African method consists in throwing a number of objects on the ground and seeing how they fall. If the objects are all alike – cowrie shells or pieces of leather, for example – the answer to the question depends on which way up they are. But many diviners have

Tablets of wood or ivory of the type used for divining
by Shona and Tswana. Each has its symbolism, and the answer
is given by the relative positions in which they fall when thrown
on the ground. The process is usually called 'throwing the bones',
though the objects used are not actually bones.

a collection of different objects each of which has a symbolic meaning, or many possible meanings, and the answer they give is arrived at by seeing how these objects lie in relation to one another. The interpretations given by such diviners resemble those offered in telling fortunes by playing-cards, the favourite method of divination in Europe from the fifteenth century.

The commonest Nyoro method is to drop a number of cowrie shells on the ground after whispering an address to them, and to see which way up, and in what kind of pattern, they have fallen. In his address the diviner reminds the shells that he is an authoritative practitioner, using the skill that has come to him from his forefathers, and may also adjure them to give a true answer. There are a number of standard interpretations of a very general nature. If the cowries, which have had the top of the shell sliced off so that they will be flat, fall with the sliced-off side upwards, the prognosis is good; if one falls on another, someone will die; if they are scattered, someone is going on a journey, and if three or more are in a line he will return safely. But none of these indications by itself tells the victim of misfortune what has caused his trouble; and it is Beattie's opinion that when it comes to ascribing responsibility each diviner makes his own interpretation of the answers given by the shells to questions prompted by his own knowledge of the circumstances or by what his client tells him.[11]

This kind of divination can also be used for the more specific purpose of assigning responsibility for a death, by mentioning names one after the other in the same way as with the rubbing-board. This is the popular method among the Shona in Rhodesia, and it is done there in the presence of persons among whom whoever is suspected is likely to be included.

The Ndembu of Angola and western Zambia regard as the most reliable of their many methods of divination the tossing of objects in a basket so that they form a heap at one side, and then seeing

A diviner from northern Angola with the basket in which he shakes up the symbols used in interpreting misfortunes. The white chalk which represents innocence can be clearly seen.

which are on top. In their case the objects are all different, and each has its meaning. Turner, who worked in the Ndembu area of Zambia from 1950–4, has analysed the symbolism of the objects used, and the metaphors in the vocabulary of divination, basing his conclusions on statements made to him by diviners whom he knew.[12] The divinatory objects are shaken up in a winnowing-basket, which is said to sift truth from falsehood as winnowing sifts grain from chaff. Turner was given meanings for twenty-eight objects used as symbols, but he has only discussed the more important ones. All diviners do not have identical collections; most have twenty to thirty objects.

These include, first, small figures of human beings and one of an *ilomba* snake, the human-headed serpent that is believed to be a sorcerer's familiar. A group of three, man, woman and child, fastened together, are called 'the elders', and may be nominated by the diviner to stand for some body of kinsmen concerned in the affairs of the clients – the chief and his kin, the village headman and his kin, or a lineage related to one client. A piece of red clay means a grudge, a piece of white clay innocence. If 'the elders' are on top of the heap with the red clay, the people they represent have a grudge which may have led one of them to attack by sorcery the person on whose behalf the consultation is being held. If they are on top with white clay, the group they represent are innocent.

A figure representing a man in the posture of mourning indicates whether a sickness about which the diviner is consulted will be fatal or not, according as it appears on top of the heap of objects or is concealed by others. But this figure, called Katwambimbi, also stands for a double-dealer who instigates others to kill by sorcery, falsely telling someone that another is seeking to bewitch him.

The very hard and long-lasting stone of a local fruit, which is slow to ripen, stands for 'a long time' and, among other things, for bewitching by means of the *ilomba* familiar, which is believed to cause a long sickness as the snake invisibly swallows its victim from the feet up. A small wooden model of a drum, associated with the drumming at the ritual to cure a person of possession by spirits, shows that a sick person for whom the divination is being conducted has been afflicted by a spirit and not by a human enemy.

Among the human figures is one representing a folklore character who vacillates, cannot make up his mind, will not commit himself or acts inconsistently. If this figure comes to the top of the heap something has gone wrong; no clear answer can be given. This can be blamed on the interference of witchcraft.

Although Ndembu diviners speak in their own persons when practising their art, they are not held to have acquired it merely by instruction. As is common in the case of mediums, a man learns that he is destined to become a diviner through a visitation of affliction from a spirit, here known as Kayong'u. As this was described to Turner by one who had experienced it, he suffered physical and not mental illness. But the ritual of Kayong'u, which was performed to cure the illness, and did do so, included the experience of possession by the spirit, manifested in bouts of trembling, and it is said to be in a recurrence of this trembling, sent by the spirit, that the diviner shakes his basket of symbols. Kayong'u also sends him a pricking sensation which, a diviner said, 'tells him to look closely'. The presence of Kayong'u in his body is supposed to be shown by a kind of asthmatic breathing or grunting.

Yet the Ndembu diviner is in full possession of his faculties, and there is no question of Kayong'u inspiring his speech. He has to find out where his clients have come from, on whose behalf, and the nature of their trouble. It is a characteristic of Ndembu consultations that they are not made by a single individual either on his own behalf or on that of one of his dependents, as is much more common. How many people make up the party will depend upon the seriousness of the trouble and the importance of the sufferer. The death of a leading man is the most serious matter of all, and in such a case all sections of the area in which he was important will be represented. If a village headman has died or is sick, someone should go to the diviner from each of the two or three sublineages making up the village, as well as a representative of people living there in virtue of affinal relationships.

While shaking his basket and putting questions supposedly to it the diviner is in fact, at each stage, narrowing down a field which

is already limited by circumstances. He must find what they want to know, but here too the field is limited, as Turner points out; nearly all consultations concern 'death, illness, reproductive trouble or misfortune at hunting'. If the matter is a death he will ask questions – expecting the answer 'yes' – about the nature and duration of the illness. Then he will identify the dead person's name. Again, Ndembu names fall into a limited number of categories by their meaning, and he begins by asking 'Does the name belong to the earth, to the trees, to the water, to insects, to animals, to fishes' going on to the sub-classes within these categories and finally to the name itself. This is the method of all guessing games. Even in countries where everyone plays these games, some people seem to have an uncanny skill at them, and in a culture where they are not an everyday pastime, skill in quickly reaching the right answer makes an enormous impression. He then finds in the same way the village of victim or sufferer. This must be within a limited area, since the people will probably have come on foot and are not likely to have travelled for many days. Then he must find the

The old man on the left is a Pondo diviner. He 'smells' witches in virtue of powers conferred on him in a ceremony of initiation, without using materials or becoming possessed. He may accuse those present of causing by witchcraft the misfortune they have come to consult him about.

relationship of kinship or affinity to the victim of each of the consultants. 'He might say,' said one informant, 'You are the dead person's older brother. This one is your youngest brother, but this one here is your brother-in-law'. As a diviner put it, he finds out 'through Kayong'u' and 'by asking questions and by mentioning things one after the other'. By this time he is in a field where his general knowledge of local gossip and of typical sources of enmity come to his aid. Now he must reveal the 'grudge' that has caused the death or sickness, by the position of the red clay in his basket in relation to the human figures; he may make the 'elders' stand for one or other sub-division in the village and see whether 'the grudge' attaches itself to them.

The significance of the presence at the consultation of members of all sections of the village is that all may know the source of the grudge that has injured their village-mate. It is the task of the Ndembu diviner – as it is not that of many others – to assign guilt, and he does so by marking one of the consultants with red clay on his forehead and the rest with white. As will be made clearer in a later chapter, accused persons and their kin rarely accept such a judgment with meekness, and it is said of Ndembu diviners, who are more specific in their accusations than many others, that at the end of a consultation they must depart in haste for fear of violence.

Somewhat similar is the process of divination of the Pondo in the Cape Province of South Africa.[13] Here too several people will visit a diviner together, and here the diviner is supposed to indicate where they come from and what their trouble is, simply by making statements. After each statement the consultants must clap their hands and say 'We agree', but the diviner has to judge from the volume of applause whether the agreement is genuine. Also there is a phrase, translatable as 'Put it behind you', which is used to indicate genuine agreement that a fact has been established and need not be further enquired into. The Pondo diviner, like the

A Nupe mallam divining by means of marks drawn in sand. The principles by which the marks are interpreted resemble those of the system illustrated in the diagram on pages 98–99.

Ndembu one, receives his first payment at the point when the facts of the situation have been elicited. But the Pondo diviner may fail in this task, whereupon the consultants go to another; it is of course possible that this may happen among the Ndembu too. If he succeeds, however, he goes on to divine the source of the trouble in the same way, judging from the manner of the stereotyped answer whether his analysis is acceptable. Like the Tswana diviner, he does not mention names but refers to categories of kin. In Monica Wilson's opinion, those who consult him have already made up their own minds who is responsible for the trouble, and, if their view is not upheld, will seek another diviner. But Turner says that in the consultation of an Ndembu diviner there are always conflicting suspicions; and this must surely be so, since each of those present is seeking to direct suspicion away from himself and his close kin.

Some very elaborate types of divination are characteristic of West Africa. One which was observed among the Dogon people of Mali (former French Sudan) has been described by the late Marcel Griaule and Denise Paulme. Here the oracular answer is believed to be given by a jackal, the animal which the Dogon believe to be the most cunning of all, the only one who could deceive God. Certain spots are treated as sacred to the jackal, and at such a place a diviner traces out in the sand a diagram which includes every factor that seems relevant to the problem brought to him. The basic diagram is a rectangle divided into sections for the sky, the earth and the underworld – God, man and the dead – and the diviner adds marks to represent elements specific to the question about which he is being consulted. These latter are drawn in such a way that their meaning is not obvious; hence the consultant cannot offer his own interpretation as an alternative to the diviner's. The drawing is left overnight, and groundnuts are laid around it to attract the animal. The answer to the question is given by the prints left by the jackal as they are interpreted by the diviner when he comes back in the morning. The traces of other creatures, such as land crabs or spiders, are used in the same way in the Ivory Coast, Nigeria and the Cameroons.[14]

Since we are dealing not with physical treatments but with grave accusations against persons, the need for an answer that will satisfy public opinion, even if it must be only a majority opinion, is clear, and one of the purposes of the diviner's questioning is to elicit this opinion. It is obviously easier to do this with the flexible methods of the Ndembu basket-diviner than with an object which is supposed to give an unequivocal yes or no. Yet where such an object is used in public, as in the Shona 'throwing of bones', the problem has to be faced. One way of dealing with it is described in one of the court records published by Crawford.[15] It is the evidence of one of two men, *A* and *G*, accused of consulting a diviner, which is an offence in Rhodesian law. *A*'s brother had died and he asked *G* to go with 'all his people' to the diviner to find the cause. This is in accordance with the Shona rule that all suspects, or at least the heads of their families, must be present at the divination. The bones were thrown, first for all the spirits who might have slain the man in anger, then for the members of *A*'s homestead. Then 'The doctor said, "Yes, the person died in your kraal" [i.e. the cause of his death was there]. I asked if he meant that I was responsible. The doctor replied that he meant one of my people'. A man *S* was identified; the doctor was asked to repeat the throw, and it gave the same result. Then *G* asked if this man was the witch and was told no, his wife. At this 'I asked the doctor if he was telling lies. I said "She is a small person and could not find medicine to kill" '. This seems to be a case where, to avoid making an accusation that would evidently have given offence, the diviner named somebody whom no one suspected. The consultants went away, outwardly satisfied, but took no action against the woman.

This Yoruba horseman carries a divining bowl on
his head. Yoruba divination is concerned
with many other matters besides witchcraft,
notably the question whether the ruler of a state
is in favour with the supernatural powers.

(*top right*) The Dogon diviner makes marks in the sand representing aspects of the matter about which he is consulted, and comes next day to see which of them have been linked, and in what direction, by the tracks of the jackal. From left to right these signs represent two spirits, an animal and a snake.

(*below*) What a diviner might find in the morning. In addition to the jackal (1), a bird (2) and some other animal (3) have left prints. A small stick (4) and a pebble (5) have been knocked out of the division of the picture in which he had placed them. In this picture the sign representing death has been destroyed by the jackal (6). The diviner makes his own interpretation.

(*centre right*) A man wants to know which of the two cows to buy. The man is represented by **1**. A pile of pebbles represents his money. The two animals are the pairs of lines **3** and **4** (simplifications of the 'animal' sign). The track **A** means 'Buy animal 4'. The track **B** means 'Buy animal 3'. Track **C** cuts off both animals and enters the division representing death. This means the animal he buys will die.

(*bottom right*) Is it dangerous for the enquirer to travel? If the jackal's tracks run from left to right (**AB**) it will be safe, if from right to left (**DC**) it will not. The four diagrams are after Griaule.

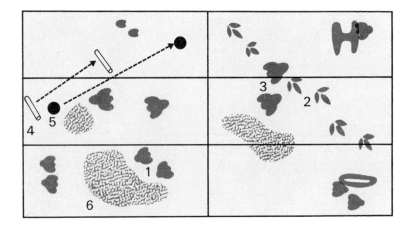

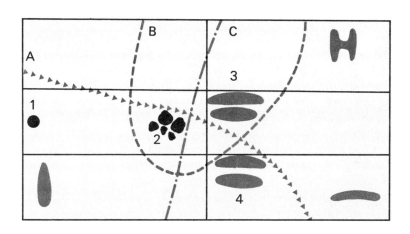

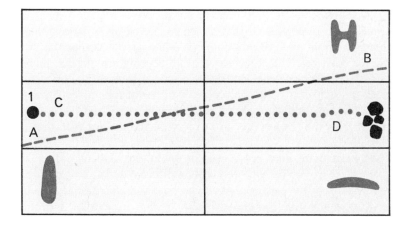

But the result of an unpopular answer can often be annulled by consulting another diviner, as it can in the case of personal consultations by using another oracle.

All African peoples have stories of the rivalries and jealousies between diviners, and there is nothing surprising in this, since it is a characteristic of most skilled professions. Evans-Pritchard[16] describes how, during the Zande witch-doctors' dance, one will aim at another a kick which is supposed to shoot a piece of bone into his body and make him ill; the other will twist round to dodge the missile, and later return one of his own. They can discomfit their rivals in other ways too. When Evans-Pritchard travelled in the Congo with Kamanga, his servant whom he had had instructed in witch-doctoring, the latter's presence was resented by the leading local expert. They engaged in a long dance of rivalry, in which Kamanga triumphed when his magic missiles caused the other man's hat and leg ornaments to fall off. More often it is said, without elaboration, that diviners injure one another by sorcery. Pondo diviners use special medicines for protection against envious rivals.

Many writers on this subject have asked whether all those who consult diviners believe in their mystical powers. The answer is in some ways analogous to that which might be given to a similar question about medical practitioners. Some people assume that the doctor must be right; a few say that all doctors are quacks; many become critical of their own medical man if they dislike his diagnosis or treatment. But people in distress must be able to think there is somebody somewhere who can help them, and the greater the distress the readier they are to rely on the nearest help that is available.

Though there may be scepticism about the skill of particular diviners, there can be none about divination as such as long as there is no doubt of the existence of witches and sorcerers. Zande witch-doctors learn the technique of appearing to extract harmful substances from their patients' bodies. It is not to be supposed that there are no laymen who suspect that this is a deception. But however many individuals may be discredited – and few are publicly discredited – the faith that reliable diviners exist if only one can find them remains unshaken. Travelled men who have lived in cities will assert that, although they have never found a reliable diviner in the place where they live, they know of one in a city a hundred miles away.

5 Suspicion and accusation

Something was said in an earlier chapter about the kind of people who may be regarded in different societies as likely to be witches. A few cases were quoted where persons in these categories were actually accused. But one cannot usually find a close connection between general ideas about witches and the direction of suspicion in particular cases, although, as some of Turner's examples show, when someone is suspected people may begin to remark on his witch-like characteristics. The Zande, as Evans-Pritchard pointed out, hold in theory that anyone may be a witch, since the operation of this mystical power is involuntary. But a Zande consulting his poison-oracle does not treat as entirely open the question of the direction whence danger threatens him, or disaster has already come; he goes over in his mind the people who he thinks are his enemies. Everybody has enemies, and these enemies must be people with whom he is in sufficiently close contact to have some cause for rivalry or quarrel; all the persons who are suspected of enmity towards particular individuals cannot possibly belong to the same category or the same section of the community. Certain classes of person, particularly those, such as clients, or wives from other tribes, who are not thought of as full members, may be vulnerable to accusation because they have no one to defend them; but many others may be accused. Indeed, it has become apparent from the observations of anthropologists that the choice of person against whom suspicion shall be directed is very much a matter of the struggle for political power at village level. At times when this is acute, accusations will be bandied between factions; at times when there are no sharp divisions, scapegoats will be found among the defenceless.

Differences in circumstances result in differences in the way accusations are made as well as in their direction. A general calamity, such as epidemic or drought, cannot be ascribed to a particular enmity between individuals. The reaction to it may be, as was indicated earlier, the performance of a cleansing ceremony; otherwise it may be the denunciation of unknown witches. But general as well as individual calamities may be interpreted as punishments justly inflicted by spirits offended by the behaviour of men. The individual calamities for which people seek to assign responsibility and seek a remedy are, in practice, sickness and reproductive troubles. Zande may ascribe to witchcraft every inconvenience they suffer, and seek to avoid it in advance, but they do not identify and accuse a witch unless the trouble is one that can be put right by the removal of the witchcraft. Peoples who believe in witchcraft also often hold it responsible for deaths. Death is irremediable, but they may take steps to avenge it. These again may be directed against a known or an unknown witch. It sometimes happens that people prefer to ascribe a sickness or death to an unknown witch rather than point to an actual person.

Alternative explanations

Except, apparently, among the Zande, witchcraft is always one of alternative explanations. In Africa, as I have tried to show, the alternative to witchcraft is deserved punishment, and this may come from the spontaneous anger of a spirit or from spiritual action set in motion by some member of the community. In this latter case the aggrieved or indignant person should withdraw the punitive influence when the sufferer has admitted his fault. But obviously – obviously, that is, to most readers of this book – a recovery will not necessarily follow. What then? Must it be supposed that the angry elder is so unforgiving that he will not revoke his punishment even when the offender has repented? If the sickness continues it must be caused by someone's unjustified malice – that is by witchcraft.

Lienhardt[1] refers to this kind of ascription of sickness to anonymous witches among the Dinka of the southern Sudan. The Dinka, though they have much to say about the characteristics of the imaginary witch whom nobody has ever seen, very seldom name a person as a witch, except on impulse in the heat of a quarrel. Like their neighbours the Nuer, they believe that most uncontrollable events are in the hands of divinities other than ancestral spirits, and they appeal to these Powers (as Lienhardt calls them) when they are in trouble. But they also believe that both justified anger and unjustified hatred can cause their object to fall sick. On one occasion a young man had fallen sick after a quarrel with his mother's brother, a man whom he ought to have treated with great respect. The older man made a sacrifice for his nephew's recovery, saying that the quarrel was now a thing of the past. But the prayers spoken at the sacrifice included denunciations and threats against the unknown witch who might be the cause of the trouble: 'If a man has hated Akol, he will get what he will get'. On another occasion when long prayers were said on account of the illness of an old priest, the divinities of his clan were called on to show their stength by punishing the witch responsible for it. But no attempt was made to identify a witch by divination.[2]

Threats against unknown witches are made in Nyakyusa villages as a preliminary step before names are named. If they are supposed to be causing some such trouble as a person's serious illness, or a fall in the yield of milk ascribed to the activity of witches in sucking the cows dry at night, then the headman of a village section, or of the whole village, will call together the people under his authority and address them. It is of course assumed that the witch must be one of them; it is hoped that he will be shamed into desisting from his activities.

But the actual naming of witches is sometimes found necessary in most African societies, the Nyakyusa among them. A witch is usually identified by divination; as we have seen, if the oracle or diviner does not point out an individual, he narrows down the field to a single kin group or household. In many cases, again as we have seen, the alternative possibilities are offered by the people who resort to the divination; and in those in which the diviner purports to discover through his own powers all the facts of the situation, he actually makes use of such local knowledge as he has, and what he can deduce from the behaviour of his clients, and selects one from a narrow range of possible answers to their enquiry.

The Nyakyusa are exceptional in that they can proceed to the naming of witches without recourse to divination, relying on the powers of the 'defenders' who see them in dreams. The procedure followed in the past was described to the Wilsons.[3] One of the 'defenders' would claim to have seen the witch; the people of the village would be assembled and the headman call out their names in turn. The 'defender' would answer 'yes' until it came to the person whom he accused, and would then remain silent. A man the Wilsons knew, who had a reputation as a 'defender', said that in such an assembly a witch could be recognised by his guilty manner. One who did not join in the chorus of condemnation, or, even worse, suggested that there was no witchcraft about, would be suspected; the person actually described as behaving in this way was already a suspect and was held to have confirmed the suspicion. It seems that a 'defender' who dreamt of an attack by a witch might rouse the village at once by shouting his denunciation, but nothing of this kind happened while the Wilsons were there.

But Nyakyusa can also follow the more usual course of examining their conscience for ways in which they may have incurred some merited punishment, at the same time as considering who has a grudge against them. The nature of such an examination, the number of possibilities considered, depends on the religious system of the people concerned; not only the types of offence that are thought to incur mystical retribution, but also the range of possible sources of such retribution. The Nyakyusa include among these the effect of general public reprobation. As they see it, when an action outrages public opinion, people begin to whisper about it, and the actual breath of their whispers attacks the wrongdoer like a cold wind and makes him sick. One section of the Nyakyusa call this force 'the breath of men', and another call it a curse. They use the same word of any direct rebuke. Such rebukes are perhaps uttered more often by outsiders to village society, such as employers or school teachers, but they are interpreted as causing the events against which they warn, such as marital unhappiness or the loss of a job. The chilling effect of 'the breath of men' can be removed, it is said, if the neighbours reveal the cause of their anger, and the wrongdoer admits his offence and makes amends by offering a feast to those he has wronged. But the Wilsons neither witnessed nor heard of an actual instance of this procedure.

Kasitile's story

Hence a sufferer may be guilty of an offence towards men or spirits, or of an offence towards his fellows which has angered the ancestral spirits. All these possibilities are likely to be canvassed in case of a prolonged illness. The Wilsons recorded one such case which extended over two years.[4] The sufferer was a hereditary priest and rain-maker, Kasitile, a descendant of chiefs and a man of much importance in Nyakyusa country. When he first became sick – possibly with tuberculosis – it was generally agreed that he was at fault. He had failed to inform his fellow priests from the neighbouring Kinga country that he had succeeded his elder brother and moved to live in the latter's home, and they were angry with him. But after a reconciliation his illness continued. He next fell ill after a quarrel with some junior priests, commoners, not hereditary

Kasitile the Nyakyusa priest, whose long illness led him to consult one diviner after another.

office-holders, over the performance of a first-fruits ritual, which consisted in an offering of beer to the ancestors of the chief. The beer should have contained certain medicines of which Kasitile was the custodian, and one pot should have been brought to his homestead for his priestly ancestors to drink. But the young priests performed this ritual without even letting him know, and he came by chance on them drinking the sacred beer. They asked him to join them, but he was too angry. Then they each sent him a shilling as a token that they begged his pardon, and he responded by buying a shilling's worth of beer and inviting them to share as reconciliation. Immediately afterwards he fell ill. Again some said it was his fault; he should have provided a far better feast. He considered that his juniors had bewitched him out of greed, but he did not directly accuse them. To his friends he said their conduct was responsible not only for his own illness but for the cold weather afflicting the whole country. He went to stay with a friend in a village where the defenders against witchcraft were said to be numerous. But this did him no good, and he sent his son to consult a diviner, at the same time maintaining that Kyala, the high god, had preserved him from actual death at the hands of his enemies. The diviner said the sickness came from two of his wives, who felt neglected and were allied with the night-witches. Kasitile consulted another diviner, Ndembwe, who agreed to come and sleep in the house and see the witches in his dreams.

The story breaks off as the Wilsons leave the country. When they return eighteen months later, Kasitile is still seeking the reason for his ill-health, but now new possibilities are being canvassed. Just before their return he had again consulted Ndembwe, whose oracle said he had 'done something wrong at home'. He guessed what it might be; he had lopped the branches of a tree growing over his father's grave. The diviner told him to make a sacrifice, and he made a rather smaller sacrifice than was suggested. His health was better for a short time. Then he decided to try another diviner further away, and this time Godfrey Wilson went with him. He offered the outrage to his father's tree as the cause of his trouble, and the diviner asked him to suggest other possibilities. He came home dissatisfied, having apparently wanted Ndembwe's interpretation to be confirmed; he preferred this to any suggestion that he had done wrong towards the living. He tried a third diviner, who suggested as an additional reason that the mortuary rites for his dead brother had not been completed. To meet this possibility he decided to instruct the dead man's son to perform the necessary rites. Yet a fourth diviner told him he had left trouble behind him

A Nyakyusa diviner rolls a lump of millet porridge in his hands. If the lump flattens out the oracle is answering 'No' to the question asked.

when he moved to his brother's homestead. At this he admitted that he had encroached on a neighbour's land, and the diviner told him the injured man had bewitched him, *but* the lopping of the sacred tree was an additional reason, and had led the ancestors to punish the whole country by making the cows abort. A bull must be sacrificed, the most costly sacrifice of all.

While preparations were being made for the sacrifice a new cause of ancestral anger was suggested – that Godfrey Wilson had been allowed to witness the rituals performed by Kasitile. But this was dealt with by a special prayer and a small offering from Wilson.

On the day of the sacrifice the beer-drinking and meat-eating which signified reconciliation were accompanied by the speaking out of grudges which, as in so many African societies, is considered necessary to make an end of quarrels and of the concealed hostility that leads to witchcraft. A number of questions unconnected with Kasitile's trouble were raised, also some grievances of older date between him and the commoner priests. But the climax of the day was an exhange of veiled phrases which implied that the commoner priests had in fact attacked him by witchcraft and that he knew it. 'They fly in their witchcraft to come here,' said Kasitile afterwards, 'they speak with the shades, saying, "Punish him! Let him find us something to eat!" They call the shades to help. Hence I sought something for them to eat [i.e. the sacrificed bull] that they should be satisfied.' This was the 'speaking out' or confession that annulled the effect of the witchcraft.

A briefer record from the Nyakyusa[5] illustrates the variety of possible causes that were considered when a man died – again not in any formal conclave but in the comments of household and neighbours. He was unfortunate before he died; his millet would not grow. He himself, it was said, thought this was either because his children were angry about something or because his wives were bewitching him. One of his wives thought the dead were angry, but suggested no reason. He then made a sacrifice, but did not distribute the meat in the village, and some thought the neighbours' indignation caused his death. His son had committed adultery with his younger wives, an act which is thought to endanger a husband. There were also two possible directions from which sorcery might have come, from a younger kinsman whom he had accused of sorcery and from a chief who claimed authority over the land where he had planted his millet. An autopsy was held to reveal that the cause was sorcery – but not, of course, where this came from.

These stories do not demonstrate that Nyakyusa go over possible causes of sickness and finally settle on one and take the appropriate action. They show, rather, that the interpretation of sickness as a visitation willed by some personalised being has the effect of a continuous review of behaviour and assertion of social norms, in which the belief in witchcraft provides an escape-route for people who are unwilling to admit that they have failed in their duty to others. Kasitile's is the story of an old man in a prominent position, whose actions could be held, because he was a priest, to affect the community at large. At certain points in the story we become aware of hostility between him and the priests of lower rank: he considers that they do not treat him with due respect, they let him know that they can contemplate mystical action against him. This particular man lived another seventeen years.

The story of Gombe

A life history recorded by Marwick during his work among the Cewa of Zambia[6] throws light from a different angle on the question of suspicion and accusation. This time we are dealing not with a single illness, but with all the misfortunes of a lifetime as they are remembered and accounted for near its end. The story is that of a man named Gombe, the headman of a village where Marwick worked.

The first disaster was the death of his two children in infancy, both suddenly, though not both at the same time. The day before the first child died a dead lizard and unnamed other objects which were thought to portend sorcery were found in the doorway of his house. Gombe, as a Christian convert, had refused to take as a second wife the widow of his mother's brother, and the result was ill-feeling, interpreted by Gombe as the widow's hatred of him and his wife. The day before the child died the widow's daughter had quarrelled with Gombe's wife. When the second child was taken ill the parents were away. It had a sore chest. This is supposed to be the affliction which automatically punishes adultery in circumstances where it is considered particularly reprehensible; it may strike any member of the guilty person's family. But this alternative, always an embarrassing one, was not considered; it was assumed that the widow was responsible for both deaths. No action was taken, however.

The next untoward incident, also a sudden death, did not affect Gombe directly. It was that of a female relative who died while he and his wife were visiting her and her husband in a mining township. They begged the husband to send her to hospital, but he refused; hence they suspected him of causing her death by his own sorcery.

At that time Gombe had been working in Southern Rhodesia. He remembered that he had had many unspecified troubles because his fellow-workers were jealous when he was made a timekeeper, and he ascribed to this the death of another child.

When he became a village headman, Gombe took a second wife, to the great indignation of his first wife, from whom he now became estranged. When a horn, supposedly containing sorcery medicines, was found in the second wife's hut, it was assumed that the first was bewitching her, although his story as recorded mentions no consequences alleged to have resulted. After a quarrel in which he struck his wife she took him to court, but he turned the tables by producing the horn, and she was reprimanded.

The next story is one of the few in the African records in which somebody is actually accused of behaving in the manner of the witch of fantasy. This person was one Jolobe, the head of a section of Gombe's village. When one of Gombe's sisters' children died Jolobe stayed away from the funeral, and he was then observed every evening to sit staring in the direction of the child's grave. The first action suggested that he was responsible for the death, the second that he was planning to feast on the corpse. Protective magic was made over the grave. Jolobe fell ill and – as Gombe tells the story – asked that whoever had made the magic should undo its effects; this Gombe could not do, so he said, because he had too recently had sexual intercourse to be able to handle the necessary medicines. His refusal was interpreted as sorcery by the members of Jolobe's section, who left the village in a body.

In the next incident we can see how the same action can be right or wrong, defensive magic or evil sorcery, depending on who is looking at it. Gombe's sister, Tapita, was ill, and a diviner told her – without being consulted – that her brother was trying to kill her, and suggested that she should pay the diviner to kill *him* – an example of the behaviour of Katwambimbi (see chapter 4). When she was at death's door she confessed this to Gombe, who prayed to God to punish him if he was in fact responsible but to let her live if he was not guilty, and she recovered. He then began to talk of questioning the diviner; whereat the sister gave the diviner more money and asked him to be quick and make away with Gombe. Tapita told Marwick that she recovered just at the moment when Jolobe died, an explanation that upheld the theory that Jolobe was responsible for the illness, and so was indeed a sorcerer who deserved to be caught by protective magic; but added that Jolobe's kinsmen were now saying Gombe had killed him *by sorcery so as to make her well.* She then produced a new explanation of her own illness; that Jolobe's mother had accused *her* of magically driving weeds from her own garden into the other woman's, and then they had quarrelled.

In Gombe's prayer we have an indication of the idea that people may be witches without their own knowledge, the idea that is thought by some writers to explain the confessions of witchcraft made in some African societies. The story also illustrates in how many different ways the theory of mystical causation can be applied, and how much this depends on the importance for individuals or groups of directing suspicion away from themselves – at least as much, I would suggest, on account of the moral stigma attaching to these accusations as from fear of physical sanctions. Although any generalised statement would describe the use of protective magic as entirely permissible, and although people who disliked Jolobe would think it divine justice that it should strike him down and so save Tapita, his friends turned this into an accusation against Gombe. I should mention that Marwick thought Tapita was inventing a story; nevertheless, she invented what seemed to her probable.

Gombe met his death in a road accident, and this too had to be ascribed to the deliberate intention of some person. Some said he had been bewitched by an elder sister who used to beg from him – as was her right in this matrilineal society, where a woman is not wholly dependent on her husband – but thought he gave too much to a younger sister. But others held that the sorcery came from a lover of his second wife, and Gombe's heir told this woman that she was 'spoiling the village' and sent her back to her own home.

This list of incidents make a story only in the sense that they all concerned one man. They are given in order to show the great variety of different contacts out of which suspicions and accusations can grow; indeed, there is no contact which cannot become the occasion of a quarrel. The dramatic events that will be told in the next chapter happened in villages where there was a crisis of authority and a division of the village was imminent. The contest was conducted largely in terms of accusations of witchcraft and sorcery. But even in these situations of crisis all accusations were not expressions of the major divisions within the villages; some concerned personal rather than factional quarrels. It is worth calling attention to this point because it has sometimes been argued that the 'function' of witchcraft – that is the most important effect of the ascription of sickness and death to this cause – is to facilitate the division of villages when the time is ripe for it.

The story of Kasitile does not bear out this theory and could not, because, as it happens, the re-organisation of villages and chiefdoms once in every generation is a recognised part of Nyakyusa tradition. The story of Gombe, although certainly a secession took place at one point in it, and although, if it were linked to other stories, one might see it as part of a factional struggle, shows that his witchcraft troubles began long before he held any political office and that most of them were not closely related to village factions.

6 Witchcraft and lineage fission

Two volumes recently published, Middleton's *Lugbara Religion* and Turner's *Schism and Continuity in an African Society*, are very largely concerned with the process of division – that is in effect the rejection of common authority – within small communities based on the principle of common descent. They approach the question from slightly different points of view. Middleton is primarily interested in religious belief, but finds that this is inextricably bound up with the religious validation of authority and the question whether mystical power is used for public, or abused for private, ends; this is the question that comes to be debated when a man begins to lose authority as he grows old, and younger men seek to assert autonomy. For Turner the central theme is the continual division and reconstruction of the Ndembu village in Zambia, but a detailed history of this process in one village shows how the relations between two sections of a village, and between the contestants for power, affected the ascription of responsibility for sickness and death.

In the African context it should never be thought that such ascriptions imply the kind of persecution of opinion that has come to be called 'witch-hunting' in Europe. We are concerned with societies in which the ability of men to manipulate mystical forces is unquestioned, in which people feel helpless unless they can find some reason when disaster afflicts them, and in which, in many cases, it is the express responsibility of the head of a kin group to ascertain the reason and take the appropriate action. What may be debated is the question whether the mystical forces have been set in motion with or without justification, but we are a long way from medieval and later disputations about the reality of witchcraft, or from the punishment of witchcraft by people who could have listened to arguments against its existence.

The witch fantasies of the Lugbara have been mentioned earlier. As was remarked in that context, they make no attempt to pin

Hut sites at Araka. In the course of fifty years, the population of Araka lineage became dispersed, though the furthest distance between two houses was less than a mile. Olimani's direct dependants moved away from Ondua's, and when Ondua died they asserted their autonomy as a separate lineage. After Middleton. See also pages 124–5 for genealogies.

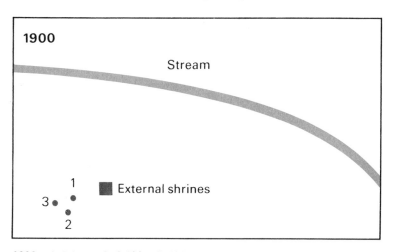

1900 1 Dria   2 Cakida   3 Abiria

1950 1 Ondua   2 Oguda   3 Draai   4 Benyu   5 Olimani   6 Okwaya
          7 Otoro and Obitre   8 Edre and Siki   9 Njima

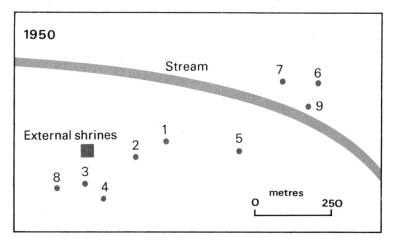

responsibility for their real troubles on persons with the characteristics of the fantasy-witch, and indeed the rest of their system of religious and moral ideas would make this impossible. The Lugbara express, more overtly than most African believers in witchcraft, the idea that witches and persons who have authority to bring mystical harm upon ill-doers both draw their power from the same source.

A Lugbara lineage divides

In order to understand the way in which conflicts of authority are fought out by means of accusations of witchcraft one must know what is meant by a lineage system and the segmentation of lineages. The Lugbara reckon descent in the male line, and remember their agnatic ancestors for many generations. Their ideal is that all male members of a lineage, with their wives, should occupy the same territory and respect the authority of a senior man, the eldest son of his predecessor. Clearly it is impossible for all descendants of a single man to form a compact group for ever, and anthropologists are beginning to reckon that a group so organised divides about every fifty years. The split is marked by the recognition of a man from a junior line as an independent lineage elder, and possibly by the recognition of a territorial boundary between seceding and parent sections. The moment of division is not reached without tension, since ideally division itself is wrong.

The settlement described in Middleton's *Lugbara Religion* was that of Araka lineage with its wives and a few unrelated dependents, ninety people in all. Araka traced its ancestry to a founder four generations back from the oldest living generation. A stream marked its boundary with two other lineages from which this founder must have separated. Araka was divided into two sections, Lariba and Nyaai, descended from, and called after, the two wives

of its founder, but all recognised Ondua, the head of Lariba, as their elder. But for a long time the junior section, Nyaai, had resented the tutelage of the senior, and when their sons grew up and began to need more land, they began to move their homesteads away from the original compact cluster. Thus the division between the two sections had already been made a fact in the spacing of their houses. Olimani, the head of Nyaai, had the duty of assisting Ondua in ritual matters, but the men were not on good terms and Ondua did not call on his aid if he could help it. Some members of Nyaai had moved their huts across the stream that was theoretically the lineage boundary, and Olimani suspected them of seeking to reject *his* authority. This then was the state of Araka lineage in 1950. The Lugbara are one of those peoples among whom authority is supported by kinship sentiment and ritual power alone; the elder can call on no coercive force. His authority is effective in so far as he can show that the ancestors, for whose worship he is

responsible, give him their support. This they do by punishing evil-doers at his request. An offence against the norms of kinship angers the elder, who is their custodian, and in his anger he sits by the homestead shrine of his dead forebears' ghosts and wordlessly calls on them to punish the offender; to utter words would be to curse him, and would have such dreadful consequences that the elder does not go so far. Sooner or later the offender or one of his family falls sick, and if the oracles interpret this as the response of the ghosts to the invocation, his authority as elder is vindicated; or, one might put it, if his authority is generally accepted, the oracle will ascribe the sickness to his invocation. An elder would never be known to have invoked the ghosts in vain, since his act is not public; nor would he be likely to, in a country where there is so much sickness.

But his claim to be responsible for the sickness might be other-wise interpreted, and it is here that we confront the Lugbara version of the Nyakyusa ideas of python power or the Tiv ideas of *Tsav*. The elder's indignation, setting in motion that of the ghosts, is held to be the cause of the sickness that attacks the offender. But the word, *ole*, which describes this indignation, is also used for much

The Lugbara 'boiling medicine' oracle. 121
Pots filled with medicated water
represent suspected persons.
All should boil over except one ;
this is the guilty one.

less admirable sentiments – for the resentment of somebody who is
not invited to a feast, or the envy of a bad dancer when he sees the
success of a good dancer; in fact, for just those feelings which are
believed to motivate witches – and it is used as often in that context.
The elder's motive should be a sense of responsibility for the prosperity and continuation of the lineage, which depends on peace
between its members. But is it always?

The story that was played out under Middleton's eyes in Araka
began, like that of Kasitile, when an old man fell ill in the cold
season; as it proved, Ondua was much nearer to death than Kasitile.
Ondua's story illustrates, as does Kasitile's, the number of alternative explanations that may be offered for sickness; it illustrates
more clearly than Kasitile's the relation between the explanation
generally accepted and the balance of opinion in the community.

In Lugbara a diviner is not expected to guess where his clients
have come from or what their problem is, and most of those consulted during this story lived very near the Araka settlement and
must have known its members well. The procedure is that the
client explains the trouble and its antecedents, and a number of
sticks are laid on the ground to represent names of possible sources.
This may be done by either the client or the diviner; if the client
selects the names, the diviner is not told whom each stick represents. The rubbing-stick, which will eventually choose among them,
is supposed to 'hear' the preliminary explanation. At a consultation which Middleton attended, names were put to the rubbing-
stick oracle twice in succession, and then for confirmation to an
oracle of another type in which medicines are heated in small pots,
and the answer is given by the one that does not boil over. The
result was indecisive, and the party returned next day. At these
consultations the names put before the oracle were all those of
people who might have had legitimate complaints against the sick
person; 'witchcraft' in the abstract was included on some occasions,

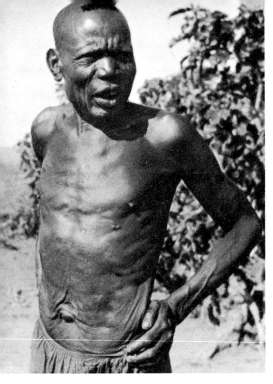

Ondua the elder, whose claims to have invoked the ancestors were denied. Those who resented his authority whispered that he made people sick by witchcraft.

but not all. If there was difficulty in reaching a conclusion, this was ascribed to witchcraft.

It will be seen that the nature of Lugbara beliefs makes it impracticable for a diviner to ascribe a sickness to witchcraft by a named person. It is his function to identify the living man or ghost responsible for the sickness, but a man so identified will claim to have caused it through invocation of the ghosts, and indeed will be anxious to be named, since this enhances his reputation for ritual power. One might almost say that people are competing for suspicion rather than seeking to avoid it. There do not appear to be occasions when someone is accused by a diviner of witchcraft against a person over whom he would not have authority to invoke the ghosts. Thus the imputation of witchcraft must be made in other ways than by direct accusation.

Olimani, the head of the section which sought to assert its independence of Ondua.

That was what happened at the beginning of what proved to be Ondua's last illness. The Lugbara method of dealing with sickness, like that of many other African peoples, is to ascertain the cause and make the appropriate sacrifice. At the sacrifice there should be a 'speaking out', such as was described in the Nyakyusa story, but much more formal in nature. The person offering the sacrifice and one or two others stands up and speaks at length, recalling events that preceded the sickness, with the ostensible aim that all present should agree on the rights and wrongs of past quarrels and put an end to resentment. Ondua was in a position to manipulate this situation so as to substitute his own version for that of oracles appealed to by persons some at least of whom were critical of him.

Olimani claimed, along with Ondua's own half-brother Oguda,

This genealogy shows the relationship between Ondua and Olimani and their respective dependants. The two sections are descended from two wives of the man thought of as the founder of the lineage. Oguda, the half-brother of Ondua, could never become the elder of a lineage, since Ondua would be succeeded by his son Yekule. It is men in his position who most commonly seek prestige as oracle operators. After Middleton.

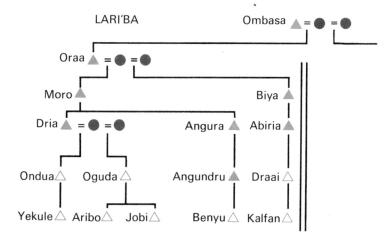

to have invoked the ghost of Dria, father of Ondua and Oguda, because Ondua ate the meat of sacrifices in Olimani's section but never made a sacrifice himself. Failure to sacrifice does indeed make the ghosts angry; it is impious, and it is the only way of flouting kinship authority that is possible for a man who is senior among all the living. His more pious relatives may well be moved by it to righteous indignation. But in this case the expression of interest in eating meat might in another context, or in other eyes, have seemed like witchcraft.

Oguda was sent to the diviner on Ondua's behalf, and so was in a position to ask whether his invocation had caused the sickness. Ondua disputed the answer and consulted his own rubbing-stick, which, he said, rejected it but would not give another one. A second consultation resulted in an explanation less damaging to Ondua's

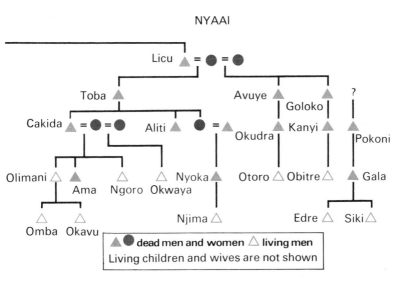

NYAAI

Living children and wives are not shown

▲ ● dead men and women △ living men

prestige: that Dria was punishing him without human prompting. Oguda, in the presence of Olimani and two others, consulted a chicken oracle of his own, and it confirmed this. Ondua told his son that the oracles had erred, but said it would be undignified for him to go on arguing; he also suggested that Olimani was actuated by *ole* (implying the pejorative sense). 'Perhaps Olimani is a witch, but I have not heard this said,' his son told Middleton.

Normally it is for the senior kinsman to make the sacrifice on behalf of a sick person, but nobody was senior to Ondua, and as he was somewhat recovered he conducted the proceedings himself. Instead of sacrificing to the angry ghost he offered a sheep to God, who in Lugbara belief alone sends death, not as a punishment but simply when the time has come, but who may 'remember' a man and let him live a little longer if the sacrifice is made. In his formal address Ondua said that the offering was made to God, but that his father Dria, who would also eat of it, was distressed at the amount of ill-feeling within the lineage (he used the word *ole*). He did not, of course, mention the neglect that others had said was the cause of Dria's anger. Thus, while satisfying Dria, he diverted attention from criticism of himself and by implication cast suspicion of witchcraft on others.

Olimani's accusation that Ondua partook of sacrificial feasts in Nyaai, but himself made no sacrifices that Nyaai men could share, was one way of asserting the separate interests of his section. A more effective one was to take the responsibility for cases of sickness in Nyaai, claiming that the ghosts had sent them in response to him and not to Ondua. When a girl was ill two months after Ondua sacrificed the sheep, Ondua claimed to be responsible after an oracle (consulted by Olimani) had ascribed the sickness to Olimani's invocation. He said that he felt (righteous) *ole* against the father of the sick girl, who had behaved with presumption. Ondua said in private that Olimani was 'destroying Araka' by his claims to independent access to the ghosts; and indeed that was his intention. Olimani retorted by hinting that Ondua was a witch and later refusing to drink beer with him. His admission to having felt *ole* was evidence of guilt, if his status as responsible for Nyaai was not accepted; if it was, he was within his rights. But even in private Olimani did not go beyond the hypothetical. 'Perhaps Ondua eats our things at night, perhaps we do not know his words . . . Who can know these things?'

On his death-bed Ondua referred, still without naming names, to the presence of witchcraft in Araka; he himself had made no accusations of this nature, though witchcraft had been put to the oracle as a possibility in some of the cases in which he was concerned. He bade his people 'hide those words and live in amity'. He forgave Olimani for accusing him of witchcraft, saying it was wrong for brothers to quarrel, a death-bed reconciliation that was more important in Lugbara than it might be in Europe, since the ghosts of men who die with grudges are believed to afflict the living. He named his son as his successor, and bade all Araka accept him as elder, and not destroy the lineage by quarrels but treat one another as brothers.

But within a few months Olimani had become independent as elder of Nyaai. An outbreak of sickness in Nyaai had been interpreted as a demand for sacrifice by the ancestors who, he suggested in veiled terms, had been neglected while Ondua was elder of all Araka.

It had indeed been clear that the division would be made as soon as Ondua was dead. But what is interesting about this story is the attitude that it reveals towards kinship and the principle of lineage unity, which will be found elsewhere as the context of accusations of witchcraft (or sorcery, as the case may be). Even where it is clear that division is inevitable, the seceding group must justify its departure from the ideal by placing responsibility on the senior line whose authority would maintain the lineage as one. It is they who must be held to have destroyed kinship. And in Lugbara, where it is possible to place opposite interpretations on what is alleged, and admitted, to be the same mystical act, it can be argued that the very man who is claiming to uphold the norms of kinship has in fact violated them.

It is also possible, within the Lugbara system of ideas, to identify the types of alternative that present themselves when the cause of a misfortune is sought. Generalised misfortunes here are ascribed to the anger of spirits and not to the malevolence of witches. Individual misfortunes may be caused by the ghosts acting by themselves, by the ghosts responding to the indignation of a living person, or by witchcraft. Sickness and other misfortunes happen all the time, but at times when a conflict of authority is acute the interpretations offered will reflect the aims of the contestants. This applies particularly to claims to have invoked the ghosts and accusations of practising witchcraft – alternative descriptions of the same conduct. To explain a sickness by the independent action of spirits is to take a neutral line, since it evades the question of the right to invoke.

This is the essence of Middleton's Lugbara story. He reminds us that people who are not contestants for lineage authority may also invoke the ghosts against their dependents. In these cases the alternative explanation of witchcraft is not called for.

The idea that righteous anger can itself provoke mystical punishment is not confined to the Lugbara, but it is not very common. Where the alternative explanations available depend simply on the question whether the sufferer has or has not deserved to suffer, the possibility of witchcraft will be much more often considered. As Turner has shown in his account of a comparable crisis of authority among the Ndembu, the direction of accusations is linked with the conflict, but at times when it is not acute they may be unconnected with it.

A Ndembu village divides

A Ndembu village is differently constituted from a Lugbara settlement. In the first place, the Ndembu reckon descent in the female line, so that in principle it is the children and grandchildren of sisters, not of brothers, who should live together. Although it is women who continue the lineage, it is men who exercise authority within the village. The rules of residence, which say that if a couple from different villages marry the woman must go to her husband's home, enable brothers, and the sons of sisters, to keep together and build up a village based on matrilineal descent. A man has no lineage rights in the place where he grows up, since that is the village of his father. Yet he does not normally come back to his

This old Lugbara man is suspected of witchcraft for two reasons : he has a squint, and his grin is interpreted as a pretence of good nature made so as to deceive.

maternal kin until his mother is widowed or divorced. He may not do so even then, if his mother has lived long with her husband and borne many children. But he may found a new village with his brothers. Those villages which do persist through several generations do so because lineage women with their sons return home when their marriages come to an end. Such a village will come to consist of two or three divisions, each taking its descent from a different sister, and it is these minor lineages whose male heads will compete for authority – that is for the office of headman, a position recognised in Ndembu society. It is held to be right and proper for people to return to their lineage home, yet they are not driven to do so by any such inducement as claims to village land for cultivation; they take into account primarily the character of the man under whose authority they will be. Men with ambition, therefore, must actively induce kinsmen from other villages to join them. It is not thought right to break up lineage solidarity by secession; this has to be justified by a good reason, and this is where accusations of sorcery are significant, as are accusations of witchcraft with the Lugbara. They may also, without leading to a division of the village, effect disqualification of a possible successor to the headmanship.

But the accusations have different consequences. The Lugbara make them reasons for rejecting the authority of old men. The Ndembu make them reasons for moving out of a village. Turner's book is full of instances where people explain moves in this way, and the same could be said of other matrilineal peoples of central Africa. In the very short space of time that I spent in a Cewa village, some people I hardly knew told me they had come there to escape sorcery; it was a matter-of-fact reason, not something people were reluctant to discuss.

Ndembu villages are very small, and Turner calculates that one with a population of fifty is ripe for division. Villages divide more often today than they did in the past, largely because men who can earn money by growing crops for sale like to set up their own 'farms' and build brick houses outside the village, away from kinsmen who might make claims on their income.

The village whose history Turner followed in detail was called Mukanza. Its founder was a famous hunter who, some time after 1913, seceded from the village of headman Kahali. His reason was that he had quarrelled with the chief of the area where the village was at that time. He proposed that it should move as a body, but Kahali refused. Mukanza died in 1919, and his next brother took his name, a sign that he hoped to become headman. But Kahali now also quarrelled with the chief, and began to consider rejoining his 'younger brothers' in Mukanza, though he did not make up his mind for ten years. The descendants of a remoter common ancestress also returned to Mukanza village from a distant area. Their senior man, Yimbwendi, who had been a headman when they were independent, also hoped for the headmanship of Mukanza, and was supported by one Kafumbu, the senior man in a numerous lineage of slave origin, who could not hope to become headman himself.

By all accounts quarrels were rife in the village, in part because there was no acknowledged headman. When Kahali finally decided to come back he also proposed that the whole village should move again, whereupon Yimbwendi said it was time for it to divide, and that he and Kafumbu, who were both tired of the quarrels, would move out together. Kafumbu in thus asserting his right to move was taking advantage of the abolition of slave status by the Protectorate of Northern Rhodesia, but Kahali's section disputed his claim, argument led to a fight, and some – not all – of Yimbwendi's and Kafumbu's sections moved out. Of those who stayed, one woman said Yimbwendi was a sorcerer and she wanted to protect her children from him; others were married to members of Kahali's section. Thirty years later it was being said that Kafumbu had killed the first Mukanza by hiring a sorcerer to shoot his *ilomba* (see p. 56), and had been named by a famous diviner as responsible for the death. But this, as Turner remarks, might well be a story later attached to an unpopular memory. Nevertheless, it is typical of the accusations made between village factions.

The village was now so much reduced in size that the government proposed to amalgamate it with neighbouring villages. Kahali managed to avert this fate by persuading the kinsmen he had left behind to come and join him. His village now consisted of the descendants of Nyachimpendi through her two daughters, having lost the Yimbwendi section descended from her sister. At first it was thought of as one lineage, which should choose its headman from the senior branch – the children of Nyachintang'a. But as time went on the descendants of the younger sister came to think of themselves as a separate lineage, the children of Malabu, who might

The genealogical links between
the leading characters in the drama
of the division of Mukanza village.

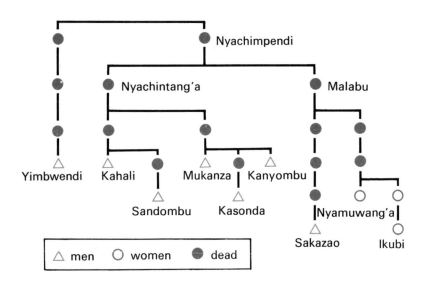

either support one of their own members for the headmanship or
secede and found their own village.

The first challenge to Kahali's authority, however, came from a
member of Nyachintang'a, his own sister's son Sandombu. In
1947, a few years before Turner came to Mukanza village,
Sandombu had deliberately insulted him, first by not giving him
the proper share of a duiker he had killed, and then by taking
possession of a bushbuck that Kahali himself had caught and sent
back to the village to be divided. In the course of recriminations
each threatened the other with sorcery, using euphemisms (in this
case the word 'medicine') which perhaps do not commit the speaker
but are understood in one way only. Sandombu said 'Some people
must look out', which was a slightly more explicit threat, and left

the village for a place where a notorious sorcerer was believed to live. It was assumed that he was going to hire this man to shoot the *ilomba* which Kahali was assumed to possess, although he had never been accused of sorcery. Kahali died soon after. Sandombu denied having made any threat, and said he only left the village for the sake of peace. But the suspicion was enough to make people say he should not succeed to the headmanship. He was already unpopular because of his ill-temper, and a sorcery suspect because he worked harder in his fields than it was supposed anyone could do without the help of familiars, and from that time he was the focus of suspicion. His quick temper certainly contributed to this, since it led him to utter threats which could be quoted against him.

A year or so after Kahali's death some fellow-villagers tried to interfere when Sandombu was beating his wife, and he said he would make the busybodies pay for it. Again he left the village, announcing as a farewell 'Tomorrow someone will die'. And next day an old woman did die, saying as she expired, 'Sandombu has killed me.' On the previous occasion no divination had been held because such practices were criminal under Protectorate law, as they still are under the law of Zambia. This time Sandombu offered to pay the fee of a diviner in Angola. Again there was no divination, but Sandombu was told to leave the village, and was absent for about a year. Meantime opinion within the village began to come round, partly because he had seemed to be genuinely sorry at the death. A divination was held in secret, and the old woman's death was ascribed to the husband of her granddaughter, who plays no other part in this story. Sandombu begged the headman to let him come back, and was allowed to. After this there was peace in the village for a few years.

The subsequent events in the story were actually witnessed by Turner, and in his account we can see the difference between direct observation and the most careful work on recollections. The stories of past accusations tell one who was finally adjudged to be the sorcerer responsible for a particular death; they do not record all the alternatives that were canvassed before this point was reached, and memories of occasions when no agreement was reached are not preserved. The eye-witness sees all this, and if he knows the society where he is working he sees how members of different groups seek to divert suspicion from themselves by directing it towards others, and how competing interests lead different sections to choose their suspects.

The first crisis that Turner witnessed himself was caused by an epidemic of malaria. Two old men had died, and Mukanza the headman and Sakazao, the leading man of Malabu, who had been spoken of as his possible successor, were seriously ill, as also was a young woman, Ikubi. The wives of the two sick men openly accused Sakazao's rival Kasonda, Turner's servant, of causing the epidemic, using sorcery medicines from the local mission hospital, which has a reputation for purveying them because it gives asylum to people expelled from their villages as sorcerers. One reason for suspecting Kasonda was that he had not come to the funeral of another old man who died a little time before; the reason actually was his work with Turner. Kasonda himself had no doubt that Sandombu was responsible, though he did not say so publicly.

Kasonda offered the alternative explanation that the spirit of Kanyombu, one of the recently dead, was troubling the village, an interpretation which exonerated himself and would make it unnecessary to direct hostility against any living person. But his sister took up the suggestion, and sought to corroborate it by saying that Kanyombu in his lifetime had drunk a kind of medicine which would enable his ghost to take vengeance on the lineage of anyone who bewitched him; this meant the lineage to which Sakazao and the young woman Ikubi, and also Mukanza's wife, belonged. Women of that lineage were reputed to acquire dangerous familiars by inheritance; this is one of the very rare references in literature based on direct observation to the practical application of a theory that witchcraft is inherited. To accept this would have meant open recognition of the enmity between the two village divisions and might have led to accusations against Mukanza's wife. Both she and Kasonda therefore rejected it, and referred instead to grievances that Kanyombu's spirit could have had against members of both lineages, for wrongs done during his life-time and for neglecting his funeral. This was where the discussion rested. Mukanza agreed to go to hospital, the same hospital where Kasonda was supposed to have got his sorcery medicines. This amounted to the withdrawal of the accusation against Kasonda, since hospitals cannot cure witchcraft. It also illustrates the in-consistencies that characterise attitudes towards witchcraft. A theory may be accepted if it is a necessary part of a specific explana-tion, but it is not extended to cover every situation to which it might logically apply.

Thus nobody said of Sandombu 'once a sorcerer always a sorcerer'. Sandombu was away from the village, as Kasonda also had been, but he had become a village benefactor in that, as a road foreman, he could give jobs to fellow-villagers. More important, however, in Turner's view was the fact that Malabu lineage, which had always been the minor branch and never provided the headman, had recently increased in numbers by the return home of several members. This made them possible rivals, hence objects of hostility and so suspicion. But it also put them in a position to oppose the claims of potential headmen of Nyachintang'a lineage, and this was one reason to throw blame on Kasonda. But at this stage the general feeling was that the village should not be divided, and both lineages could accept an explanation of Mukanza's sickness in which both shared the blame but neither was accused of the ultimate wickedness.

The young woman, Ikubi, did not recover. Before she fell ill an old woman, called Nyamuwang'a, her mother's sister, who had been accused of witchcraft more than once, had asked for a share of some meat she was cooking, and when she said she had none to spare, had been angry and was said to have used threats. Ikubi's father at once accused her of killing his daughter, and after very little discussion she was told to leave the village. When she had gone her hut was burned down. Ikubi's father, who had been living in the village of his wife's lineage because he was afraid of sorcery in his own, returned home, saying the sorcery was worse in Mukanza. In this case the death of a young woman is treated as an isolated incident. She was not an obstacle to anyone's ambitions, and her death was not made an occasion for recriminations between rival lineages. Responsibility was pinned on a person of no significance in village conflicts, to whom suspicion had attached before, who was quarrelsome and unpopular and who had no son to defend her and reject the accusation. But Sakazao, the head of Malabu lineage, who turned her out, said he was angry at the dissension within the lineage and did not commit himself to the accusation. With her daughter and granddaughter she went to live on Sandombu's farm, a little settlement that Mukanza people were wont to refer to as 'that village of witchcraft'.

Although headman Mukanza recovered from his serious malaria, he was a very old man, and everyone was speculating on the future of the village after his death. Sakazao was confident that he would become headman of a united village, arguing that he had never been accused of sorcery as had both his possible rivals, Sandombu and Kasonda. Kasonda said there was too much ill-will between Sakazao's lineage and his own; he was planning to start a farm near the main road, and might do this even before Mukanza died. He would take with him the members of his own subdivision of Nyachintang'a, a lineage by this time big enough to divide.

This very rich material shows that accusations of witchcraft and sorcery are not always connected with rivalry for authority, but that conflicts for authority commonly employ such accusations. The majority of the Ndembu accusations are concerned with responsibility for death, which, it will be remembered, is ascribed by the Lugbara to God and not to human activity. By holding a contender for office responsible for causing or attempting the death of his predecessor his rivals can debar him from the succession, but one does not find here that such accusations are made in order to justify the rejection of an incumbent's authority. The headman in office was never accused, though this happens in other central African societies. Nor does one find the division of the village community treated as a rejection of kinship norms so serious that the equally serious offence of witchcraft must be invoked as a justification for it; division is too easy and too frequent in a society where people are not anchored by their claims to land for cultivation. What one finds is that the association of witchcraft with a quarrelsome nature and the harbouring of concealed grudges supports the ideal of amity in the village, and does occasionally lead to the expulsion of individual trouble-makers. It is natural for people to dislike their rivals (or their husbands' rivals) and it should not be supposed that accusations are made in cold blood to further political aims; at the time when they are made they are believed by those who make them. And since the accused know they are not guilty, it is natural for them to offer alternative explanations. The special interest of Turner's account is that it is based on public discussion and not on the consultation of oracles. He shows also how accusation may be retrospective; that is, how some time after the event the ascription of a death to some individual's witchcraft will come to be a part of village tradition. Thus, although the question of responsibility for Kanyombu's death had been shelved when it was agreed that Kasonda had not killed him by sorcery, it was later taken for granted that a woman of the rival Malabu lineage had bewitched him.

From these detailed studies one can see how differently in practice people make use of a belief the roots of which are everywhere the same: that disaster is caused by the purposive action of humans or personalised non-human beings, and that those who harbour unjustified resentment are the most likely human cause. For the Lugbara it was a way of expressing resentment against a man who had lost his personal authority, and of interpreting as illegitimate actions which he claimed to have taken in virtue of his right to call on the ancestors. For the Ndembu it was sometimes no more than the means of assigning responsibility for a general disaster and thus supposedly removing the cause, but at other times it was a weapon in a minuscule struggle for power. The direction of accusations reflected the state of public opinion at different times, and animosity against individuals fluctuated with this. Nowhere in these stories was any person unequivocally and finally condemned.

7 The treatment of witches

When Mary Kingsley visited the coast of Angola in 1893 she saw in Kakongo 'several unpleasant-looking objects stuck on poles'.[1] These proved to be human lungs and livers, and it was explained that they had been taken from the bodies of dead witches whose guilt had been confirmed by autopsy, and were displayed as a warning to the general public. Did these gruesome exhibits come from people who had been convicted of witchcraft and put to death, or from people who after death had been found by autopsy to have the physical characteristics attributed to witches?

Nothing is harder than the attempt to judge how persons found guilty of witchcraft were treated in the days when tribal authorities were not subject to any external restriction. The laws of Zambia and Rhodesia impose heavy penalties for the imputation of witchcraft, and for claiming to be able, and also for trying, to perform witchcraft (sorcery in the anthropologist's sense); they also penalise the consultation of diviners. Hence divination can only be practised in secret, and cannot have the quasi-judicial function that it had when the diviner publicly marked the guilty and acquitted the innocent. The naming of a witch renders any person liable to three years' imprisonment, and for a professional diviner the penalty is seven years. Nevertheless divinations are held. The Ndembu go to Angola for them, but in the other cases I have quoted nobody crossed a frontier. Diviners practise in Buganda, though their activities are frowned on by the African administrative chiefs who are responsible there for law and order. In Bunyoro, although the official attitude is the same, accused persons are openly tried in the chief's court – formally not for committing sorcery but for claiming to be able to – and the chief has their houses searched for sorcery objects, and sends them to prison if any are found. But the execution of a sorcerer or witch would be murder; moreover, in Africa today only the highest courts can pass sentence of death.

There are then limitations on what can be done to rid the

community of witches. I use this phrase because I believe that this, rather than punishment for a specific act, is the significance of the reaction of African societies towards what they consider to be proof of witchcraft; in African tradition other offences, even homicide, could be atoned by the payment of compensation. From what is said in Africa today one might conclude that witches, if identified, were invariably put to death in the old days, and that since this was prohibited witchcraft has everywhere been on the increase. But one also hears that women were always faithful in the days when their husbands could kill adulterers.

The treatment of witches in the past

Some quotations from the anthropologists whom I have taken as my principal sources show how differently the past is described today among different peoples:

In ancient times habitual sorcerers were tied up in dried banana leaves, which are highly inflammable, and burnt to death; it is said that in Mukama Kabarega's reign, during the latter years of the nineteenth century, many sorcerers were despatched in this way. (Nyoro, Beattie)[2]

In Ndembu custom a person divined as a Katwambimbi [the trouble-maker, see chapter 4] receives the same punishment as a sorcerer or witch, i.e. in the past death by burning or ostracism from Ndembu society with confiscation of property. (Turner)[3]

In pre-European days vengeance was either executed directly, sometimes by the slaughter of a witch and sometimes by the acceptance of compensation, or by means of lethal magic. Witches were very seldom slain, for it was only when a man committed a second or third murder or murdered an important person that a prince permitted his execution. (Zande, Evans-Pritchard)[4]

The execution here took the form of a revenge killing by the kin of the victim, not of joint action by the whole community. Possibly this may be correlated with the fact that to the Zande witchcraft is a quality that anyone may have, and not something monstrous.

Formerly when a man was convicted of witchcraft and did not admit it, he was compelled to move from his village, and often to leave the chiefdom altogether. Often his cattle and crops were taken by the chief . . . A wife convicted of witchcraft was commonly divorced . . . Rarely was a supposed witch killed.   (Nyakyusa, Wilson)[5]

Munya was killed by the people of Mokedo for his witchcraft activities. The circumstances of his death illustrate the kind of spontaneous action which, formerly, could be taken against witches. When Munya was passing one of the Mokedo hamlets, he was asked to come in and rest since a bush-pig was about to be roasted and eaten. He entered the homestead and sat down. A fire was kindled, and three stakes were bound together as supports. Then someone said, 'Everything is ready; bring the pig.' Munya was seized, tied to the stakes and thrown on the fire.   (Mandari, Buxton)[6]

Van Valkenburgh is undoubtedly right in considering witchcraft as a crime for which the Navaho administered capital punishment. A considerable number of witches put to death are referred to in the literature, and a much larger number are known to me from reliable white and Navaho informants. Sometimes, when tension mounted sufficiently, the witch was killed without 'trial', sometimes by an aggrieved individual but equally often by a group of relatives (and friends) of some supposed victim. The manner of execution varied, but was usually violent (by axes or clubs). Shooting at the hands of injured individuals occurs fairly often. I have heard only once of hanging.
(Kluckhohn)[7]

The only one of these statements which makes any attempt to be quantitative is Kluckhohn's. He has the advantage of records going a long way back. Jean Buxton's dramatic account of one incident shows what the Mandari could do, but tells us nothing about how often they did it. The others show that, at any rate in the memory of Africans in the past thirty or forty years, the past treatment of witches differed very much in different places. One might ask, however, whether a generalisation about the past can ever be taken as applying to all cases without exception, and suggest, as a contrast between Africa and Europe, that the wholesale executions of witches of which historians tell us were carried out by judges to whom the accused were strangers, and that in a small village community, where it is dangerous to accuse a person because he has friends, it may be all the more dangerous to put him to death. But this is pure supposition. We have to content ourselves with the knowledge that the restrictions introduced by colonial law have certainly had some effect, although we cannot be quite sure what it has been. Beyond this we must do what we can with the observations of anthropologists among peoples subject to this law and aware of its penalties, and from these one can certainly say that today this is not a matter of detached diagnosis or judicial sentence leading to only one possible conclusion, and then wonder if it ever was.

Ordeals

An essential element in the traditional treatment of accused witches that has been almost everywhere suppressed is the administration of ordeals. Ordeals are supposed to cause death or serious injury to a guilty person who undergoes them; and if they do in fact do so it is hard to conceal this from the authorities.

The test about which most has been written is commonly called the poison ordeal, the drinking of medicines which an innocent person is supposed to vomit. It does not follow that everyone who fails to vomit the poison is killed by it; in fact there is plenty of evidence that this is not so. Nevertheless, people sometimes are. Accused witches were not always obliged to undergo the ordeal; they might demand it to clear themselves, confident that they would be able to do so. Among the Nyakyusa accused and accuser drank together; either party could be represented by a kinsman, and it was said that they would choose a member of the family who vomited readily. Sometimes the aim was to decide an issue between groups of kin, in which case the result could not lead to action against an individual. The convicted person did not die in any of the cases which the Wilsons' informants remembered.

A very different account is given by Mary Douglas[8] of the effect of the ordeal among the Lele of the Kasai in the former Belgian Congo. Like the Wilsons, she was able to talk with people who had witnessed and even been subjected to poison ordeals. She tells us that the administration of the ordeal was effectively suppressed about 1930; Monica Wilson said that the last case of which she heard was in 1932. One is on record in Northern Rhodesia in 1953. The Wilsons' records were obtained in 1938; Mary Douglas was among the Lele in 1950. She was told that there used to be many ordeals and many people died; and a number of her case-histories refer to decisions by ordeal. Her account is concerned with sorcerers who are supposed to be responsible for the death of their fellows. Every death, except that of very old men, is supposed to be the responsibility of some member of the community, and this person is supposed to pay compensation. Adulterers are held responsible for the death of women in childbirth and of infants, sorcerers for the rest. Hence, Mary Douglas argues, the kinsmen to whom the compensation is due have a strong incentive to identify an individual as guilty. But, as she remarks, there are nevertheless always two opinions about an individual's guilt, his close kin refusing to believe the accusation; this is very much what has been illustrated in detail in the story of Mukanza village. She tells us that they reject the accusation because they cannot believe that someone they know well and regard with affection has done the outrageous things ascribed to the fantasy witch. This may be, but it would be interesting to have Lele statements to this effect. In the detailed stories from which the two preceding chapters have been taken, expressions of suspicion rarely extend the field of discussion beyond reasons for ill-will to corroborative evidence from behaviour, observed or imaginary. It is true that logically a witch in many places must have killed a close kinsman in order to become a witch, but most accounts do not give the impression that accusations are held to pass a retrospective judgment on the accused person's whole life. Nevertheless, it is easy to understand that an accused person's kin resent accusations against him and seek to direct suspicion elsewhere.

The Lele are like other African peoples in their confidence in the justice of the ordeal; a person who submits to it expects to clear himself. The alternative is to accept the unpopularity that follows a number of accusations and, of course, attracts more; this may reach the point where the unpopular person is driven out of the village despite the support of his kinsmen, who remain resentful at the treatment given him. While Mary Douglas was there an old diviner who was held by the European courts to have poisoned one of his patients, and convicted of manslaughter (not murder), was ostracised by every village on his return and had to live in the bush, where food was secretly brought him by sympathisers.

The ordeal, as it is described today, put an end to ambiguous situations; an accused person was either cleared or executed by the poison itself. It was not, however, administered *ad hoc* whenever an accusation was made. Like the Nupe *ndakó gboyá* dance, which purported to get rid of all witches of a village in a single day, Lele ordeals were held at intervals, and all persons who had been accused drank the poison at one time. Those who survived were cleared, and had to be compensated by their accusers, and the kin of those who died met all claims for blood-compensation. The men who administered the poison drank it first 'to show their fitness to perform the rite', that is their innocence of sorcery. Were they expected to vomit? We are not told. One would certainly like to know more about this poison, since it seems that in this ordeal, unlike all others that have been described in any detail, *everybody* who did not vomit died. This contrasts with one of the interpretations offered of the ordeal in Zambia, namely that the person who does not vomit first is afraid he will die and so driven to confess; the detailed accounts do not mention confession. Mary Douglas tells us that in 1959, when Belgian authority broke down in the Kasai, the ordeal was reintroduced, and that hundreds of people are reported to have died from it.

We do not know nearly enough about the substances used in these ordeals. The same word – *mwavi* or *mwafi* – is used for the poison drunk over a wide area of east and central Africa, but of course it does not follow that the substance is the same in all cases, given in the same quantity or prepared in the same way. A study of poisonous plants in Zambia[9] mentions two plants that are used, both described as containing poisonous alkaloids.

Some peoples, for example the Kaguru in central Tanzania,[10] have medicines which are believed to make people ill if they tell lies after drinking them. Other ordeals which are often mentioned are those which require an accused person to plunge an arm into hot water or fat, to walk over hot ashes or lick a hot iron. Although these have received so little discussion, they are much more terrible than the poison ordeal as it is usually described. Less well known is the Ivory Coast ordeal, in which a drop of the latex used for arrow poison is inserted into the accused person's eye. This is exceedingly painful, and seriously damages the eye unless his tears flow copiously enough to wash it out. Denise Paulme states that most people prefer to admit guilt. She quotes a statement from a Bete 'sufficiently detached from [traditional] custom to be able to judge it'. His mother's brother was accused of killing his father, and he writes: 'The man whom today, to please the majority, I take no shame to call "sorcerer" was yesterday called "my uncle".' He describes, as a hostile observer, the dance of a witch-finder, which among the Bete is supposed to mime the activities of the sorcerer to be accused: 'accusation, calumny, stirring up quarrels and family strife . . . When my uncle was accused the crowd howled at him.' He was then submitted to the ordeal, 'this dumb judge who cannot even question the accusers'. He lost the sight of his eye and 'the crowd howled at him again'.[11]

This is the statement of a man who has been taught to reject the whole complex of belief in sorcery and in the means of detecting, countering and punishing it. One guesses that he returned to the village for his father's funeral and was horrified to find that suspicion rested on his mother's brother, to whom, as his account makes clear, he was deeply devoted. Was there a conflict of lineages here? It seems that the village as a whole, or many people in it, welcomed the witch-finder's selection of the guilty man, but his statement shows what must always be the reaction of friends of the person accused.

One can say at least of the poison ordeal that it did not condemn everyone who underwent it; and there are records which show that some people can walk over hot ashes unscathed. All persons who believe in ordeals and oracles believe that they cannot lie, or at least that good ones do not lie; they believe that they are appealing beyond fallible human judgment. But since the corpus of witchcraft beliefs ascribes to the witch infinite powers of evil, there is room here too for doubt. In the main it is oracles that witches are believed able to tamper with. But I record, without any attempt at explanation, a case noted by an anthropologist recently in north-eastern Zambia. A man was alleged to have undergone the boiling water ordeal a few days before the anthropologist saw him. His arm showed no mark of any kind. He said he had successfully passed the test; others said his witchcraft had defeated it.[12]

The treatment of the guilty

What then do we know about the way witches are treated now that it is impossible to put them to death? In Turner's story of Mukanza village, a man and a woman were formally accused of sorcery and witchcraft respectively, and expelled from the village. Both returned soon afterwards, the man being received with a formal ceremony of reconciliation, marking the reluctance of the community formally to exclude a member. When the story ends the two are together in a new village, unpopular and sneered at, but not molested. Sandombu, the sorcerer, in an incident not recounted in the previous chapter, successfully brought a slander case against a man who later accused him of another act of sorcery.

For obvious reasons the ascription of sickness to witchcraft or sorcery calls for a different response from that of death. In the first case there is a situation needing remedy; in the second all that can be done is to affix responsibility, and unless this is to be followed by vengeance it is no more than a relief to the emotions of the bereaved. In case of sickness the aim of the sufferer and his friends is to have the cause removed; and where the sickness is ascribed to justified anger it is taken for granted that the anger will be forgotten when the victim has begged pardon. The Nyakyusa ritualise this belief by a feast of reconciliation at which the sick person begs pardon, and his neighbours say that their anger is over and express their good wishes for his recovery. Logically this could not be expected of a witch, the figure called in to explain a sickness that does not yield to confession and reconciliation. Yet this is possible, and is indeed the practice of the Zande. It might be argued that this is possible only in the logic of their system, which holds that witchcraft substance can act without the knowledge of its possessor. But, as already mentioned, despite this theory Zande expect those who bewitch them to be men with grudges against them.

Zande, as has been mentioned, place their main reliance on private oracles, in particular the administration of *benge* poison to chickens, rather than on the identification of witches by a person claiming special powers of detection. Moreover, their oracles tell them when disaster threatens, so that they are warned of witchcraft even before it has struck. A man who has received such a warning then places before the oracle the names of all the men whom he can think of as likely to wish him ill, indeed the same people who would probably suspect *him* of causing *their* troubles. It is for the oracle to tell him whether the list is complete. When trouble comes the witch responsible will be selected from this list; in view of the method of consultation, this is likely to be a name repeatedly offered to the oracle, hence that of a man much in the thoughts of the victim. He may then ask the oracle whether he should openly confront this person; no doubt his hesitation on this point will be a matter of the standing of the man he has it in mind to accuse. If the oracle advises against, he makes a public declaration that he is being bewitched, that he knows who is responsible but that he will not shame this man by naming him, and asserts that he has done nothing to give any neighbour cause for enmity. One reason for adopting this method is the idea that a witch who is directly accused may merely be angry and increase the power of his witchcraft. In practice, action is taken always in case of sickness, but not often in the many other situations in which Zande believe that witchcraft is at work.

Unless he is warned against it by his oracle, a victim of witchcraft proceeds to accusation, but this is still done in an oblique manner without direct confrontation. The method is to send to the man supposedly responsible for the sickness the wing of a chicken which has died from oracle poison. This action, however, requires the approval of the political authorities. The accuser should take his story to a prince or his deputy, and get from him a messenger to deliver the chicken's wing to the witch. When he receives it the witch normally says he had no idea that his witchcraft had caused injury to the sick man, to whom he wishes no ill. As evidence of good will he blows a spray of water from his mouth over the chicken's wing, a gesture that signifies reconciliation and the dismissal of anger in many African countries. He also begs the witchcraft inside him to desist from its activity. In this context the theory that witchcraft is involuntary exonerates him from moral blame, though it is hardly consistent with the fear of offending a witch that makes his victim hesitate to identify him. If the sick man does not recover, other witches are tried, or renewed appeals are made to the original one. But here there is no question of public denunciation or punishment.

In the case of a death from witchcraft the kin of the dead person have the obligation of seeking vengeance. But they must first ascertain from the oracle that this, and not magic employed to counter witchcraft, was the reason for his death. If it was witchcraft he has been murdered, and vengeance is a duty. In the old days the man held responsible might be speared, or might agree to pay compensation for his supposed homicide. But according to Evans-Pritchard's informants, it was only when the oracle had found a man guilty of several murders that the prince would allow him to be killed in revenge. Because of the importance of these cases the prince's own poison oracle was consulted. Under British authority revenge by killing was of course not allowed, and Zande have had to fall back on what had traditionally been the alternative, the employment of vengeance magic, the medicines for which are known to the 'witch-doctors'. Vengeance magic is believed to be infallibly just; if it is used after the death of someone who did not deserve to be avenged, it will return and destroy the man who sent it out. Its employment is secret; one can only tell, by seeing that the kin of dead men are no longer observing the customs of mourners, that they believe some other death has been the result of their vengeance. This too must be confirmed by the prince's poison oracle. If the oracle indicates this as the cause of the second death, there should be no vengeance for it. But the kin of the second dead person will certainly wish to seek vengeance, and will not have been present at this consultation. We do not know how Zande reconcile this opposition.

The other people on whom we have detailed information are the Nyakyusa. The first step taken by Nyakyusa when they think witchcraft is at work, the gathering of villagers to complain about what has gone wrong and beg the undiscovered witch to desist from his activities, is intended to give him an opportunity to confess. This would be taken as evidence of repentance, and of an intention in future to use his mystical power as a 'defender', and in the past, it is said, he would then not be turned out, but simply fined for the damage he had done. One suspects here that the past is again being idealised; there are good reasons of more than one kind why people should not confess. But the wish that they should do so is one with the idea that witchcraft is the expression of concealed resentment, and that people should not nurse hidden grudges but admit them and then forget them.

In the detailed stories of past cases that were given to the Wilsons, one man was found guilty by the ordeal of making the cows go dry, and was driven from the village. Another was suspected of causing the sickness of a neighbour's child. Before he was named, but when he was already suspected, the villagers threatened to drive out the man in question if he did not desist. Doubtles knowing he was suspected, he asked a friend why this particular illness should be picked on when many children in the village were sick. His proper course would have been openly to face their suspicions and either admit guilt or demand trial. 'Whispering' – talking only in private – was evidence of his guilt. He was asked to leave the village, but went to another section, where the headman did not know what had happened. His former neighbours went to the headman there and protested, and the headman told him to go.

A suspect might also be invited to leave without any formal confrontation; the message was conveyed to him by barricading his door with thorns. Or a token was set up outside his door which did not impede his entrance, but had a clear meaning. Then, it was said, people would begin to talk openly about his witchcraft and he would be shamed into leaving. This was a joint action of the village community; an individual could not do it on his own responsibility. This is rather painfully like what happens in small communities that are too enlightened to believe in witchcraft.

In many places the responsibility for a death is publicly discussed at the funeral, and accusations of witchcraft are made in a heated atmosphere. Jean La Fontaine[13] mentions such a discussion among the Gisu of eastern Uganda. Usually agreement is not reached, since kinsmen related to the dead person in different ways have contrary views. No public action is taken as a result, but any bereaved person is at liberty to credit the next suitable death to his vengeance magic. Winter[14] writes of the Amba on the Uganda-Congo border that the life history of the dead person is recounted in detail, with special attention to events just before his death, the names of persons suspected of bewitching him are mentioned, they are allowed to answer, and at the end 'there is almost complete unanimity'. Angry threats are uttered against those on whom suspicion has rested, but Winter does not mention any further action. The Logoli of western Kenya deal in another way with suspicions and accusations at funeral gatherings. One of the elders has the recognised task of maintaining peace among the mourners, and reminding them that we must all die in the end, something that all the peoples we are discussing recognise when they are not themselves sick or bereaved.[15]

Although the laws of all colonial and ex-colonial territories make it an offence to accuse a person of witchcraft, it has already been made clear that people constantly do so. In some places, as with the Ndembu, they only have to avoid letting the matter come to the ears of the chiefs whose courts are now subject to external control. In others, as with the Yao of Malawi, chiefs discuss witchcraft accusations informally outside the court house when their official business is over. In others, as with the Nyoro in Uganda, the law that it is an offence to claim magical powers is invoked against persons whom the Nyoro believe actually to have such powers; in others again, as with the Shona in Rhodesia, people make accusations on the results of divination and find themselves facing criminal charges.

Witchcraft is in fact associated with quarrelling, not with naked midnight revels or keeping pet snakes. It is malice and hatred, and not sinister mystical powers, that disrupt the small community and that the villagers want to drive out, not foreseeing that they must endlessly return. We have evidence that witches were sometimes killed when Africans were free to deal with them as they pleased; also statements that they were sometimes dealt with in other ways. We have the stereotyped complaint that colonial governments allow witchcraft to flourish; and against this we may set Monica Wilson's wise comment that 'in pagan thought Utopia is a society without witches'.[16] We may ask whether feeling against a supposed witch was invariably so strong as to lead to killing.

Apart from Evans-Pritchard's account of the Zande, we know very little, even from contemporary Africa, about what is done to witches suspected of causing minor harms; it would seem that they remain in the limbo of suspicion and gossip, as indeed it seems they did in sixteenth-century England.

Monica Wilson's conclusion on the treatment of convicted witches, both before and under colonial rule, is what one might expect from the detailed story of Mukanza village. 'The punishment seems to vary . . . with the status and personal popularity of the accused.'[17]

Again we see the illogicality that is indispensable if the belief in witchcraft is not to destroy the small communities who look to it for their preservation. If witches were indeed the hideous beings of fantasy their existence could not be tolerated. But they are ordinary neighbours, perhaps universally unpopular, perhaps with friends as well as enemies. If every natural death were to be followed by the death of a witch held accountable for it, the community would come to an end.

One finds, then, that people who have been accused of witchcraft continue to live, and may even derive advantages from their reputation. A Nyakyusa witch is turned out of the village where he is supposed to have committed his crime, but he is not rejected elsewhere. His new neighbours are not concerned with what he did in the past. Or his former neighbours may go and fetch him back, arguing as rationalisation that repentant witches are good 'defenders'. Only if their behaviour is such as to make them unpopular again is the past remembered.

Evans-Pritchard was at first surprised to find that men whose reputation as witches was known for miles around might nevertheless be citizens of standing, and even members of a prince's council. One such man, Tupoi, was his neighbour. A long list of murders and other injuries was confidently ascribed to him. People did not like to build their houses near him, and they avoided letting him know of their plans lest he should blight them; or if they could not manage this they used to try to get him to bless the enterprise (a polite way of saying, not bewitch it) by blowing water on the ground. But there is ambiguity here too. The innocent blow out water to demonstrate goodwill; witches can bewitch with their spittle. How is any given action to be interpreted? This depends upon the

The apparatus of a Nyoro diviner.
He wears the necklace ;
the gourd with stopper contains
medicine ; the rattle is shaken
to induce a state of trance.

actor's reputation and how people feel towards him at the time. A suspected witch profits from his reputation because people are afraid to offend him. They make sure to remember him when beer is being passed round or meat is brought in from hunting, and treat him with respect even if they do not feel it.

Sandombu's position in Mukanza may be compared with this. He gave many people cause to dislike him and was debarred at one time from becoming headman, thus failing in his earliest ambition. He had to build up a following of his own, outside the village, and to swell their numbers he took in a suspected witch, her daughter who was a prostitute, and a scapegrace boy who was suspected of sorcery because he threatened to kill other boys when he quarrelled with them. His new settlement was spoken of with contempt by people in Mukanza. But on the other hand, Sandombu had found work for Mukanza people when he was a road foreman. His crops did well, and even if this was ascribed to his employing spirit familiars to work on it, prosperity does command respect. He did not himself regard his farm as a separate village, and Mukanza people did not formally treat it as such, but allowed him to take a leading part in public discussion of Mukanza affairs. It was only when he let it be seen that he was again hoping to become headman of Mukanza that the existing headman mentioned 'two villages'. His reputation for sorcery was often discussed, but only in the context of general dislike for him.

The old woman Nyamuwang'a too, although she had been held responsible for several deaths, had been beaten up and turned out of the village, also, as has been mentioned, was later made a representative of Mukanza in connection with a death in another village. Pertinent here is a comment made by Crawford in a discussion of the Shona: 'Killings by witchcraft are usually soon forgotten, it is the killings by violence that become part of tribal or family history'.[18] Most anthropologists who have witnessed the reaction to a death say that the survivors are in great indignation at the time; later they may be readier to admit that we all must die, but this reflection does little to allay the indignation at a physical homicide. However, when a leading man dies, the name of the sorcerer held responsible becomes part of tradition: this shows how closely in these small societies accusations of sorcery are bound up with competition for authority.

It must always remain impossible to say with any confidence how persons adjudged guilty of witchcraft were treated in the days when it was not murder to put them to death. Allowing for this it still seems safe to say that there were many possible reactions, and that these must have depended on the state of feeling in the community, the status and personality of the accused, and the importance of the supposed victim. It should not be forgotten, moreover, that in most ages of the world's history death has been held to be an appropriate retribution for causing death, and that those who believe deaths are caused by witchcraft do genuinely believe it; they are not wilfully rejecting a truth that is within their reach. But lest it should seem that I make too little of the unhappier implications of this belief, I quote a statement from one of its most recent students:

It is very easy to discuss wizardry accusations in the clinical atmosphere of a sociological study, but it is as well to keep in mind the emotions of hate and terror, the feelings of doubt and of certainty, the moments of rationality and irrationality which accompany an allegation and of the brutality which may eventuate. I have only once personally played a part in one of these dramas, but it is something I shall not easily forget.[19]

In reaction against the stereotyped ideas of Europeans in Africa, who point to the belief in witchcraft as the ultimate evidence of African irrationality, anthropologists from Evans-Pritchard onwards have argued that it is by no means irrational in the context of the African's limited understanding of causation, and that so far

from being a sign of barbarism it has its place in a system of religious beliefs which uphold social norms. Some have gone further in ascribing valuable functions to it, and have maintained that it facilitates social change in the form of village or lineage fission when the time for it is ripe. This view, along with other theories on the significance and nature of witchcraft beliefs in small-scale societies, will be discussed in a later chapter. In this context it seems pertinent to remark that one is not obliged, because one finds these beliefs explicable and even in a certain sense necessary, to consider them beneficial. Of course it is to be regretted that people are put to death for something they cannot have done, and that judgments are based on a test as wholly arbitrary as the poison oracle. Nadel, discussing witchcraft in yet another area of Africa, the Nuba hills in the Sudan, said the belief that a man was

A nineteenth-century imaginative picture
of a Zulu diviner teaching his craft
to a number of young warriors.

159

likely to bewitch his sister's son allowed people to blame on witch-craft a relationship that was difficult because of the rules of the society, and so blinded them to the possibility of reconstructing that part of the social system.[20] I doubt if many would follow him in the implication that difficult relationships between categories of kin could be improved by deliberate action, but it is as well not to ascribe beneficial consequences to an institution simply because it exists.

8 New ways to deal with witches

Anthropologists always find themselves in a difficulty when they talk about 'the old' and 'the new'. No anthropologist can know a small-scale society as it was in the days before freedom of action in some fields had been curtailed by colonial law and new circumstances had created new possibilities of action in others. The peoples who have supplied most of my examples have been among the most remote from such new influences, but no African society has been able to ignore the colonial laws which limit the application of penal sanctions, whether against witchcraft or against other breaches of social norms. In the previous chapter I tried to show how difficult it is to judge what actually was the treatment of persons supposed to be witches or sorcerers when there were no such restrictions. It is absurd for us to pretend that what we can see now is 'the traditional' or 'the old', and this is the more absurd the longer the period during which these societies have been subject to influences from outside Africa.

Nevertheless, some part of what we see consists in processes and actions which are clearly not part of a century-old tradition. To take a rather trivial example, Tswana sorcerers began at a certain point to buy caustic soda in trade stores to use among their medicines. This gave their sorcery – when it consisted in adding medicines to the victim's food – a greater effectiveness than it had had before. The original night-guns cannot be older than the introduction of gunpowder, though that came into central Africa with the Portuguese long enough ago. Now that they are made of metal and shoot metal missiles, using, it is supposed, scrap metal from the railway lines, the shooting of one sorcerer by another acquires a new reality. The large-scale investigation of such shootings that was made in 1956–7 by the government of Northern Rhodesia could never have been undertaken in an independent African society. Life in great cities is something for which rural traditions give no precedent. New defences against witchcraft supposedly revealed to prophets constantly appear; they can certainly be called new since we know the dates when these prophets have arrived in different countries, and sometimes when they are supposed to have received their revelation. It is more open to question whether the success of the spirit mediums who have been described as proliferating in Bunyoro and in Ghana is to be regarded as a response to a new situation. But the long journeys that Ghanaians make in such numbers to famous spirit shrines would not have been practicable before they could travel in lorries. The appearance of possessing spirits not purporting to be those of ancestors, and endowing their mediums with the power of divining witchcraft, which is described both in Bunyoro and in north-western Zambia, is certainly new. One can also speak, in a sense, of new circumstances when believers in witchcraft do not take enough care to keep on the right side of the new law, and their cases are tried in court.

Many students of society believe that the desire for utopia, for a world without sin, without hatred, without quarrelling, without witches, has grown stronger in the small-scale societies since their way of life has been invaded by the institutions of the machine world. Of Africans in particular it has been said that, torn from a world they understood, full of witches though it was, they now think they are victims of witchcraft *more often* than they did in their traditional homes. This is a quantitative statement which it would be hard to verify. Frequently it rests on no other evidence than the phrase, which is certainly constantly heard, 'The witches are increasing', with the supporting argument 'because the government will not let us punish them'. It is salutary to reflect that when in 1559 Bishop Jewel preached before Queen Elizabeth I and urged her to introduce stricter laws against witchcraft, he too said the evil was increasing.

Writers on West Africa in particular have commented on the

proliferation of new shrines dedicated to spirits who protect their
devotees against witchcraft, and have attributed this to the malaise
felt by people who are experiencing social changes of bewildering
rapidity. Thus Fortes, who conducted a social survey of Ashanti at
the end of the Second World War, in 1948 described the new shrines
as 'the most dramatic symptom of the increasing sense of social and
personal insecurity'.[1] Denise Paulme observed among the Bete,
a forest people of the neighbouring Ivory Coast, that, although
their religious observances were meagre by African standards, they
were endlessly preoccupied with protection 'against the enemy'.

A Niaboua witch-finder from the west of the Ivory Coast.
His fly-whisk is an emblem of authority : the horn
is his means of communication with the spirits.
He looks in a bowl of water and sees the faces of
witches whom he has met in nocturnal gatherings.

She ascribed this, at least in part, to the upheavals of the last fifty years and the feeling that they are surrounded by undefinable dangers that their fathers never knew.[2] Yet 'the unknown by which they are threatened from all sides and at every moment' is surely just what appeared to Evans-Pritchard as the Zande picture of the accustomed world.

Then there is the argument that the fear of witchcraft has increased because traditional ways of dealing with it have been made illegal. Certainly when Africans are actually living in new surroundings, in the large towns to which so many migrate temporarily and some permanently, it is even harder than it is in the country for them to consult diviners and identify witches without falling foul of the law. Mitchell has also argued that this makes it harder for them to take action in the face of misfortune. This assumes that in the rural areas the identification of a witch was always followed by action. He quotes a case from Salisbury in which a man's serious illness was interpreted by different diviners as due to the jealousy of workmates, to the anger of his father's ancestors because he had not attended the mortuary rites of kinsmen in Nyasaland and of his mother's because obligations towards her kin had been neglected. No diviner would name the witches, and his family sought to propitiate the spirits by making sacrifices.[3] But, except in so far as most people prefer explanations which exonerate themselves, one cannot say that they were forced to accept this alternative by the circumstances of town life. In another case, cited by Crawford, a Rhodesian (Shona), a 'police boy' in a railway compound, where most of the employees were from Zambia or Malawi, was held responsible for a death and denounced at a public meeting. The men who denounced him were prosecuted, but he was moved to another depot, which had been the object of their action.[4]

One can distinguish three new types of activity concerned with protection against and deliverance from witches: the cult of spirits or talismans which are believed to prescribe remedies, the witch-finding activities of itinerant prophets, and the rituals of many of the new churches which have broken away from those established by Christian missions. A prominent feature of most of these is the performance of some act that is held at the same time to reveal a witch, to protect an innocent person and to strike down in the future anyone who is guilty of witchcraft after performing it. In many cases the act consists in drinking a medicine which may be compared to the ordeal, except that all those that have been analysed have been shown to be quite innocuous. But other methods exist: Simon Kimbangu, the prophet of the Kongo in the neighbourhood of Kinshasa, baptised his converts in a river and detected the witches among them by the way the water ran off their hair.

Talismans and spirit shrines

The cult of talismans or spirit shrines is typical of parts of West Africa. Those that have most prestige are either believed to have come from foreign parts, where magic is strongest, or to be mani-festations of previously unknown spirits. It is ironical that while M.J. Field found in Ghana shrines of 'gods' – material objects said to have been brought from the Ivory Coast – the Tetegba cult that Denise Paulme observed there was alleged to have come from Ghana.

The Bete talismans shown to Denise Paulme were generally said to have been recently bought by their owners at times when they thought they were in need of special protection, if 'all the family felt ill' or there had been a number of deaths. The method of defence is that of most protective magic: the sorcerer who attacks the possessor will himself suffer. But the next step is less usual; the talisman may also be appealed to as an ordeal. One may suppose that the afflicted person accuses an enemy. The latter can then clear

This object is used by the Bete of the Ivory Coast as a protection of the house and its inhabitants against witchcraft and sorcery. It is personified ; a person accused of sorcery may say 'If I have wished so-and-so harm, may Kéké kill me'. People strike the little bell to attract the attention of Kéké.

himself by saying 'If I wished you ill, may the talisman punish me'. If he is lying he will fall ill and not recover till he has compensated the victim of his sorcery.

Denise Paulme also refers to confessions – not, it is true, confessions of having caused harm, but of having felt resentment. She visited the shrine of a new talisman – or fetish, or god, if other words current in West Africa are preferred – called Tetegba, said to have been brought from Ghana by Baoule tribesmen who possessed and sold the secret. The medicine of protection was dispensed in a ritual resembling in many ways the Catholic Mass. A priest of Tetegba stated, in the course of a police enquiry into a death, that every sin committed in the village should be confessed to Tetegba and his pardon sought by making an offering. A person who supposed himself bewitched would take the enemy whom he suspected to the shrine, and there, it seems, he would be forced to confess and to get rid of the 'bad spirit' in which resentment is personified. The headman who in 1954 had brought Tetegba to the village where Denise Paulme saw his shrine died suddenly in 1958, and the villagers lost faith in his protection. But two months later they had found another cult.[5] The inevitable loss of faith in one panacea accounts of course in part for the constant appearance of new ones. Goody[6] has remarked that new cults are noted while the disappearance of earlier ones does not attract much attention.

The Ghanaian 'fetish' shrines described by Field[7] were very similar. The devotees drank medicines or performed some other act which gave them protection as long as they did not themselves do harm to others; moreover, the protection had to be renewed periodically and gratitude expressed in the form of thank-offerings. These shrines could be very profitable commercially, and without denying the strength of the demand for protection, one must recognise that this is an incentive for the appearance of new ones.

The most detailed description of new shrines of spirits is that made by Field, who spent some months in daily attendance at shrines at Ashanti.[8] The mediums of spirits, like those in Bunyoro, represent a new development of a long established tradition. A medium is supposedly possessed by a spirit that wishes to speak through him; this is the way in which priests were called to the service of the traditional gods. The distraught person is taken to the priest of an existing shrine, and eventually reveals the name of the spirit that has seized him. The objects in which the spirit's power is embodied are believed to fall from the sky, to be captured by a diviner and put in a brass pan which becomes the shrine; this is the traditional way of entering on priesthood. Today a new medium has to pay a considerable sum to an existing priest for recognition, but he is allowed to begin work and so earn a part of this from the thank-offerings brought after a year's protection. Here there is a striking contrast with the Nyoro *mbandwa* mediums, who are frowned upon by the strongly Christian chiefs. In Ghana they are classed as 'native medical practitioners', and a successful shrine becomes the focus of a new village. It may deal with more than a hundred cases in a day.

Field made a record of the business brought to the shrines she visited by over two thousand people; this included the presentation of thank-offerings – which, however, implied seeking further protection – as well as requests for help. Nineteen of the thank-offerings were for the death of an enemy. Most of the complaints were of 'failure to prosper' in one way or another. Failure in hunting is an old complaint, which could always have been brought to diviners. In the days when the swollen shoot disease of cocoa was at its height farmers were consulting shrines in large numbers. Field makes the interesting point here that the failure of a crop could be ascribed to a number of possible causes, some being acts displeasing to spirits or to the earth itself, which is venerated in West Africa. Witchcraft or sorcery would nevertheless be given as the explanation in the majority of cases.

In the new situations of urban life and wage employment these alternatives are not very plausible. It is to the circumstances of village life that standardised explanations in terms of one's own wrong-doing apply; though it has been shown that even there they are not often readily accepted by the victim of misfortune. Field remarks that many Ghanaians enter into employment, or undertake commercial ventures, with little idea of what this will imply – of the expectations of the employer, of the need for careful calculation if a business is to pay, of the cost of living in a town. Then the difficulties that occur are inexplicable. These are specific troubles, not the general malaise that writers are wont to assume as a consequence of social change, but they are troubles, like sickness or drought, for which no technical explanation is available. In one of Field's most interesting cases a petty peculator was being blackmailed; he ascribed his trouble neither to his own misdeeds nor to

168

A Nupe vendor of medicines.

the wickedness of the blackmailer. He seems to have seen the latter as he might a snake that had bitten him in the village, as an instrument of the envy of his less fortunate kinsmen.

Confessions

One of the most striking observations made at the Ashanti shrines was that numbers of women came to them in order to confess to acts of witchcraft for which they believed the spirit of the shrine was troubling them. This is one of the rare cases in which the belief in involuntary witchcraft has found a practical application. Field's explanation is that these women are sufferers from involutional depression, and she argues that, if this disease was absent, misfortunes would be explained in terms of sorcery rather than witchcraft. But we no longer attach as much importance as we once did to the idea of sorcery and witchcraft as alternatives. From Yoruba country, where a witch-finding cult was recently active, we learn that some old women spontaneously denounced themselves; a layman's explanation was that the pressure of the public feeling that there must be witches somewhere, along with a belief that one can be a witch without knowing it, is enough to account for this. And clearly a person seeking a ground for self-accusation could only choose witchcraft in a society which believes in witchcraft.

Possibly confessions of this kind are more to be expected where it is believed that people may be made into witches unwittingly or against their will. Some of the women whose confessions Field heard in Ghana said other women had given them their witchcraft; in effect their confessions were accusations. From the Bete in the neighbouring Ivory Coast Denise Paulme quotes more circumstantial confessions.[9] A man who had been accused told how a friend came every night knocking at his door to call him to meet the spirits of his dead parents. When he finally went out to join his friend the latter taught him the movements of a dance, and when he had learned them said 'Now you know the witches' dance'. Others said malicious people had mixed witchcraft substance with their food. Who can be sure, Denise Paulme asks, that he is not a witch? That he is not in fact responsible for the death of his own mother? The Bete, moreover, believe that confession automatically entails absolution.

An unusual form of the belief that witchcraft can be implanted in an unwilling person is that of the Shona in Rhodesia. The Shona ascribe witchcraft almost entirely to women, and they believe that if repeated misfortunes attack a woman or her children this is a sign that a spirit wishes to make her a witch. There is a ritual by which the spirit can be transferred to an animal, but if the misfortunes continue there is nothing for it but to accept the witchcraft. In the context of such beliefs witchcraft may be thought of as a disease for which confession is the preliminary to cure.

But no story of this kind is told in the confessions quoted by Crawford[10] from the records of police enquiries in Rhodesia. The aim of the Rhodesian Witchcraft Suppression Act is, of course, not to suppress witches but to suppress Africans who purport to be able to identify witches, and some of these dramatic statements were made in the investigations preliminary to trials of witch-finders. The police could have no interest in securing them under pressure.

One statement came from the trial of a woman accused of murdering another woman's child, apparently in revenge for the death of a child of her own. Muhlava, the mother of the murdered child, declared that she, the accused woman and a third woman were all witches and went about at night, riding on hyenas, to bewitch people. She described how she herself had been initiated into witchcraft as a young girl and had later initiated the accused woman, and how together the three had killed Muhlava's husband

and then dug up and feasted on his corpse. The police went so far as to exhume the body, and found no indication that it had been tampered with.

Three other women were accused of attempted murder by administering medicine to the husband of one of them, who the police thought might have been poisoned. They did not deny this, although they asserted that they had poured it down his throat when he was asleep, an action notoriously impossible. One of them told of her initiation by the others, and of joining them in naked nocturnal dances. The three pointed out to a European and an African policeman the trees to which they hitched their hyenas and the cave in which their familiars (not previously mentioned) lived. They are reported to have invited the court interpreter to their home to teach him witchcraft.

Another – this time, it is true, when accusing another woman of witchcraft – said that the two together had eaten three dead children. Yet another said that she and her sisters had used the blood of a dead child to make a love potion and had then eaten the body. On this occasion they said they had cut the body in half, and in fact the police, who were prosecuting for infanticide, had found only the lower part.

Whatever the explanation of these confessions, it cannot be the exaggerated searching of conscience observed by Field in Ghana, nor is there here any explanation in terms of an offer of absolution. The suggestion made by Crawford, who collected these cases, and made to him by Africans, is that the women who make them seek to be feared, as suspected witches and sorcerers are apt to be; also that where a number make the claim, any one will be protected from violence by the popular fear of revenge from the others. But there is one forced confession among his records. The prophet of an African church, having denounced a woman, held her in the fire until she confessed; his motive, Crawford suggests, was simply to ensure that his skill in divination should not be questioned.

From Tanzania there is record of an actual murder case in which two women and a man were convicted.[11] They described how the dead man had been killed and parts of his body divided among a number of sorcerers. The man, who confessed to the actual killing, said this had been imposed on him as a test for his admission to the company of sorcerers. All three said they had been summoned by a woman who was their leader (who for lack of evidence was not charged). In this story there is no cannibal feast; the flesh was said to be used for making sorcery medicines or to eat, but no one confessed to having eaten it. The victim was neither an enemy nor a close kinsman of any of the accused; the murder was committed, it was said, in honour of a famous diviner who had recently been killed in a road accident. Apart from minor details, none of these accused confessed to anything impossible.

Witch-finding movements

The appearance of itinerant witch-finders in central Africa was first described by an anthropologist when Audrey Richards in 1934 witnessed the arrival in a Bemba village of a party of men calling themselves Bamucapi.[12] They came from Nyasaland, and their name is derived from the Nyanja word *kucapa*, meaning to wash clothes. They had already covered five hundred miles to get to Bemba country, and they were to continue into the Congo and Southern Rhodesia. On arrival in a village they summoned the headman to line up his people, who were then made to pass behind a witch-finder while he looked in a mirror; this procedure recalls the method of divining by looking in water which is practised in West Africa, but which one does not hear of in other parts of the continent. A man who was judged guilty by this means was ordered to produce his evil charms. Large numbers of objects were produced, mostly animal horns containing substances of one kind or another. The witch-finders purported to know when sorcery objects were being concealed, and ordered searches to be made in specified places. Confession was followed by absolution through the administration of a small dose of a soapy kind of medicine; this, it was said, gave protection but would punish with instant death anyone who was guilty of sorcery after drinking it. Yet another way of ensuring that guilty persons would not escape was the threat that the witch-finder would return by night and summon witches and sorcerers to their destruction by the beating of a drum. Among those who drank the medicine were some old women who came long distances to clear themselves of suspicion against them. The villagers were delighted at the denunciation of people they had always suspected.

This is the only occasion on which an anthropologist has examined the objects surrendered by persons accused. The results were surprising. They included large numbers of ordinary domestic containers and some protective charms. Less than a dozen could be unequivocally recognised as intended for harmful purposes. Yet the villagers had been impressed by the mere size of the heap, and shuddered at the thought of the horrors from which they had been saved. In later purges of this kind, the possession of bottles or tins of patent medicines, such as anyone coming home from employment in town might bring with him, has been taken as evidence of guilt. Later accounts by detached observers make more of the implication that some objects are planted.

The Bamucapi were succeeded in 1947 by a prophet named Bwanali, with whom another anthropologist (Marwick) had a conversation in December 1947.[13] He had a permanent centre where sick persons came to be treated and stayed for some time, and regarded himself primarily as a healer but also, like the traditional diviners, as a fighter against witchcraft. He himself stated that he had brought his disciple Mpulumutsi back to life after he had been killed by witchcraft, and that he told his patients who confessed to witchcraft that they would be ill if they returned to it. He did not claim, at least in this short interview, to have himself risen from the dead. Some of the mythology originally attached to the Bamucapi was revived in connection with this movement, in particular the belief that at some future date the witches would be summoned to their destruction by the sound of a drum.

The reputation of the two healers evidently rested on the belief that they had unmasked and destroyed great numbers of witches. Nobody had seen the corpses of the guilty who had died on the way home after drinking the protective medicine, but one had seen preparations to bury them, another said so many had died at Mpulumutsi's village that the paths to it had been closed because of the stench of the corpses; and so on. The same desire to believe that evil has been destroyed accounts for the readiness to suppose that the horns surrendered to the Bamucapi had all been used for nefarious purposes. One of the more touching comments was, 'All those who are witches are going to die, and the people will live in great peace. They will develop friendships, and evil will be a very rare thing.'

But in less than twelve months people had realised that stealing, adultery and sickness – thought of as all belonging to the same category and all curable by the new medicines – were as prevalent as ever, and were calling Mpulumutsi a charlatan. Like the Bamucapi before him, Mpulumutsi was suddenly 'just not there'. This must be the fate of every movement that promises the impossible, whether with intent to deceive, as Marwick suspects of the Bamucapi, or in good faith as he judges Bwanali and Mpulumutsi. But hope does not die, and there is always the possibility that the next witch-finder will be the genuine one.

Bwanali's counterpart in the present generation is ChiNg'ang'a ('the great witch-finder'), also a Malawian, who had his head-

quarters in Karonga in northern Malawi, and carried on his operations in the more permissive atmosphere of a state where the head
has himself asserted that his opponents have practised witchcraft
against him. ChiNg'ang'a was visited, as are the Ghanaian mediums,
by people who sought his advice on many matters, but one of his
major activities was the detection of witches, which he did not by
mechanical means but by his own power. To inspire him or 'open
his mind' a chorus sang while he questioned those who came to
consult him; if the matter was witchcraft, suspects and accusers
were present, and after some talk ChiNg'ang'a identified the witch,
and turned him over to attendants who cicatrised his cheeks and
forehead and rubbed medicines into the cuts. This supposedly cured
him of his witchcraft, but it also marked him as one who had been
found guilty, and one wonders how this affected the direction of
suspicion next time his neighbours were concerned over a sickness
or a death.

ChiNg'ang'a could be invited to cleanse a community, and was so
invited to the chiefdom of Muyombe in neighbouring Zambia in
1961, when the old chief was sick and was disturbed by the new-
fangled notions of his juniors and the activities of a nationalist
political party. The headman of every village in turn was summoned
to bring his people to the chief's court to be tested. Only staunch
adherents of the Free Church refused to come, but the majority
even of its members accepted the test. A large number of unimpor-
tant people were 'cut' by ChiNg'ang'a, but also village headmen
who supported the chief's deputy and younger rival, and the
chairman of a local committee of the nationalist party.[14] He
eventually had to give up his village in Karonga because it was
suspected of harbouring politically undesirable persons.

We have less information about witch-finding movements in
West Africa, but Morton-Williams has described one such among
the Yoruba.[15] Like so many of the new ways of dealing with

witches that have been described in this chapter, it had originated a long way from the place where it was observed. The Atinga cult, as the Yoruba called it, came to them from southern Ghana, and it had come to the south of Ghana from the interior of the country, where the people are not greatly concerned with witches. The centre of their religion is the cult of the earth, and Atinga is said to have been derived from this cult when it was brought south by migrant labourers. Its devotees entered Nigeria in 1950. Their leader said he had himself brought the cult from Accra and established it a few years earlier at his home in Dahomey. Like the *ndakó gboyá* in another part of Nigeria, they visited places to which the chiefs invited them, and detected witches by dancing. The invitation could be prompted by popular demand; in one town there was a riot against chiefs who did not want them to come. Unlike the *ndakó gboyá* they were not disguised and made no pretence to be anything but human beings; in this respect they were more like Zande witch-finders and some others in West Africa. In Yoruba country all witches are supposed to be women. Men may be sorcerers, but they do not seem to have been identified by the Atinga dancers. Those who were pointed out were mostly old women, who either confessed or were tested by an oracle of a simple kind well known in West Africa: a chicken was killed and the answer given by the way it fell. If the oracle denounced them they were again required to confess, to pay a fine, and surrender objects used in sorcery. Some of those handed over were beads used for divining or 'gods' from household altars. According to Morton Williams some women were tortured to make them confess, and two were said to have been beaten to death. In a town of 10,000 population, 483 witches were recorded by the town chief as denounced by Atinga.

Morton-Williams talked with some women who had been accused. Some said they had no idea of being witches but 'supposed they must be'; some that they had been made witches against their will and were thankful to be now 'freed'; one that she *now* knew she was responsible for a number of deaths.

Divination of witches in the independent churches

Modern witch-finders in West Africa owe less to European culture and specifically to Christian ritual than do those of central and southern Africa, where it is not always easy to draw a sharp line between witch-finders and the prophets of the many independent churches. There is of course the formal one, that a church organisation must be registered in order to hold property. The witch-finding activities of the Bamucapi were marked by elements of Christian ritual, including the preaching of sermons; Bwanali, according to Marwick, thought of himself as called to combat evil in the Christian sense as well as sickness – or did not distinguish them – and his followers believed he had risen from the dead with a message from God. Simon Kimbangu, the Kongo prophet, made his name as a witch-finder before he founded his church. The independent churches of what Sundkler has called the 'prophet' type are greatly concerned with healing by means of divination, and one attraction for their members is that they join to Christianity this central feature of traditional religion. Sundkler amusingly describes the meeting at a stream for a ritual of purification of a Zulu woman diviner and the prophet of an independent church, each with followers and both parties performing the same sequence of actions. Indeed he goes so far as to say that those churches *are* 'modern movements of witch-finders'.[16]

Divination need not, of course, result in the denunciation of witches, and should not if these churches are to keep within the law. Nevertheless a Shona prophet in Rhodesia, well aware of the risks run by pagan diviners, was sure that his church was immune because the government 'knows we are with God'. In fact Christian prophets have been charged under the Witchcraft Suppression Act on several occasions. A difficulty for the Christian diviners is that since they are precluded from ascribing sickness to the wrath of the ancestors, they can offer no other explanation than witchcraft. But they denounce witches in other contexts than that of sickness. Murphree, a missionary working in the Ntoko Reserve in eastern Shona country, has described the methods of the John Maranke Apostles, who entered Rhodesia from the south in 1938.[17] Before the annual communion, for which a large congregation gathers at a specially built camp, there is a general identification of witches. On the evening before the service the worshippers enter a special enclosure through a number of gates at each of which are stationed two prophets – church officials held to have powers of divination and to detect unconfessed sin of any kind. All persons whom they denounce are taken to a 'judgment fire', where church elders hear accusation and defence. Those accused of witchcraft, if they confess, are required to surrender their horns; if not, they are merely turned out of the camp. People say they learn which prophets are most perceptive – or most suspicious – and try to avoid their gates.

According to Murphree large numbers of women confess, but sometimes an alternative explanation is offered of the sin that a prophet purports to have detected. For example, the husband, not a church member, of an accused woman may have bought a harmful charm. Some elders say they judge by the demeanor of an accused woman when she is asked to confess, but there is no room here for the kind of questioning that traditional diviners use. Nor is there any occasion for it, since the prophet is not asked in this context to account for some specific trouble.

A very different view of the prophets is taken by Crawford; he considers that they are simply replacing the traditional diviners, in any case in the eyes of those who are not members of their churches. He quotes two cases in which a prophet was consulted about a sickness, and made an accusation after dancing in the manner that has been described so often in this book; in each of these, it may be noted, the prophet ordered the accused woman to produce her nocturnal steed, in this case an ant-bear.[18]

Adult baptism necessitates confession, and this to Shona means less an undertaking to lead a new life than a magical cleansing from pollution. A person guilty of witchcraft cannot be baptised unless he confesses, and if he does not do so the prophet may denounce him. Hence some people regard baptism as a kind of ordeal and bring suspects to be tested by it. The same prophet who on one occasion divined witchcraft and so refused to baptise a woman, on another made suspects enter the pool in which converts were baptised, and apparently used this as a means of divining.

9 Fantasy and reality in witch trials

The account I have given of witchcraft in Africa is built up from the observations of men and women who have lived in African villages, heard what Africans say and seen what they do. Of course they have not seen what Africans did when they were not constrained by laws imposed on them from outside. Opinions differ as to the effect of legal constraint on African behaviour in the face of witchcraft. Certainly it is harder than it used to be to deal with supposed witches by direct physical violence, and it is not easy to guess how much this has affected the reaction to individual cases. Are we to suppose, as many Africans and some anthropologists tell us, that in the past every witch who was detected was put to death either by the ordeal itself or by a chief's orders or by indignant fellow-villagers?

The question is significant partly in connection with theories which argue that the belief in witchcraft is in some sense good for the peoples who hold it. I shall discuss these theories later. At this point I would merely express the view that it was not as terrible in its consequences as is often supposed.

What surely remains unchanged is the *everyday* quality of witchcraft to the African, as indeed of sorcery to the Melanesian. When people are not telling fireside tales but going about their daily affairs, they are not obsessed with fears of something monstrous; they simply recognise that they have enemies and had better look out for them. So do we. Occasionally one finds, as in a recent account by a French missionary from an unspecified part of the Ivory Coast, that Africans themselves believe their society is riddled with suspicions and enmities from which European society is free.[1] This, I suggest, merely shows that from a distance Europeans in Africa seem more solidary than they really are; or that, because quarrels are so distressing in small communities, they are selected as the explanation *par excellence* for what is actually a technological, not a moral, inferiority.

In Africa the belief in witchcraft is not an excrescence on or a deviation from the accepted body of religious and moral ideas; it is an intrinsic part of them. It belongs, it is true, to the more magical side of the magico-religious complex. That is to say, it is not among the actions thought to be punished by the spiritual guardians of the moral order. Except in so far as generalised prayers for protection can be held to refer to witchcraft among other ills, the defence against an undetected witch is magical, therefore man-made; you can protect yourself by charms, the ancestors will not punish him on your behalf. Nevertheless, the condemnation of witchcraft is part of the moral code; it is disapproved as an underhand way of paying off scores, whereas direct physical reaction to an injury is not condemned. Witchcraft, as a crime impossible to detect by everyday means, is treated differently from other crimes, and the ordeals which traditionally provided one means of detection could inflict great physical suffering. But the person found guilty, unlike the fantasy-witch, is an ordinary human being, and if he is punished it is for what he is held to have done, and not for being intrinsically unworthy to exist.

Granted that we can never know how witches were dealt with in the old days, I would offer the suggestion that this was a matter of the degree of popular indignation against them, and that only the death of an important person, or a series of deaths, would lead to the execution of the witch. This would parallel the killing in revenge for a physical homicide which in many African societies is a duty to the dead, and the execution of murderers by the authority of the state which is characteristic of more highly organised African societies and of many others in the world. We hear often of the burning of witches, and I have quoted one recent instance vouched for by an anthropologist. It may be that this is considered to be the appropriate punishment because it destroys the witch completely, though one does not find statements to that effect. But it is not a

Episodes in the story of the North Berwick Witches.
They were supposed to have conspired against
the life of James VI of Scotland, who was protected
against them by the strength of his Christian faith.
Illustration from *News from Scotland*.

mode of execution reserved for witches. Audrey Richards recorded, as part of the life-history of an old Bemba man, a dramatic incident when he, as a page at the royal court, witnessed the burning of some men who had offended the paramount chief. 'Did I try to help the young men my fellows?' he said. 'You ask if I pleaded for them. No indeed, I was running to fetch the firewood.'[2]

But one need not necessarily assume a public execution. There is one reference to a witch who would have been 'burnt in her hut'. There is nothing easier than to set on fire the thatched roof of an African hut; indeed it is one of the commoner forms of revenge.

Again, the ordeals, conceived as they are as a means of getting at the truth, are cruel in a context of much cruelty, from the beating of wives to the mutilation of thieves and adulterers, and much physical suffering that has to be endured because there is no remedy for it. They are imposed only on suspected witches (and sometimes their accusers), but not with the idea that witches deserve exceptional cruelty.

It would be nonsense to say that witchcraft in Africa is a crime like any other; most of the instances given in this book illustrate the attitude towards witchcraft as a particular kind of crime which calls for particular kinds of action. Nevertheless, it is a crime among other crimes. It is something that ordinary people do when they let envy and resentment get the better of them. It is not something abominable and horrendous, to be spoken of only with bated breath; on the contrary, my own experience in a not particularly witch-ridden society was that the subject might crop up in any casual conversation.

When one turns to Europe, one is presented in the best-known literature with a picture that is based on folk-lore but has moved from folk-lore to something much more sophisticated. The fantasy picture of the witch has been systematised in manuals for the guidance of judges and inquisitors, and witch trials are described as

determined attempts to secure, by confession under torture if there is no other way, evidence that the accused person has not only been guilty of murder but has also consorted with the Devil in obscene and blasphemous rites and sexual embraces. Indeed a witch in Europe need not have been guilty of murder; the North Berwick witches who were accused of conspiring for the death of James VI of Scotland (and I of England) were foiled by the strength of his Christian faith, and succeeded in nothing more than raising a storm while he was at sea. European witchcraft is not, like African witchcraft, a part of generally accepted religious belief. To the up-holders of the established faith, in which it is no longer required to fill a moral gap, it is a repudiation of religion and an alliance with its enemies. The famous trials of witches in Europe are in fact trials for heresy. It is unbelief, not uncontrolled resentment, that they seek to destroy.

This is the impression to be gathered from the standard works, most of them by writers who look backwards with the eyes of sceptics on the errors of the past, and are consumed with generous indignation at the thought that people should have been tortured and burnt at the stake for crimes of which they manifestly could not have been guilty. The centuries of spectacular trials, from the fifteenth to the seventeenth, have been described by more than one writer as the age of the 'witch craze'. They ask how it came about that in a society with a tradition of logical reasoning, philosophical speculation and legal argument, and one, moreover, which had earlier rejected the reality of witchcraft, learned men could believe something so patently ridiculous.

Their writings are there to show that they did believe it. But what has been obscured by the famous trials, either of heretics or of persons accused of conspiring against princes, is the possibility that to less exalted people the belief in witchcraft was very much what it is in Africa, an explanation of misfortune in terms of the ill-will of neighbours, and that most of the trials of witches were concerned with situations of this kind.

The writings of George Gifford, a Puritan Elizabethan clergyman who was sceptical both of the powers attributed to witches and the claims of the 'cunning folk' – whom we know in Africa by the name of diviners – are a famous source of information on attitudes towards witchcraft in the Essex of his day. His two books are *A Discourse of the Subtill Practices of Devilles by Witches and Sorcerers* (1587) and *A Dialogue Concerning Witches and Witch-crafts* (1593).

Gifford did not question the existence of witches, though he thought far too many people were wrongly accused. Indeed he thought they deserved to die – not, however, for the harm they did but for their dealings with the Devil. One of the Devil's impostures, as Gifford saw it, was to claim responsibility for many natural disasters which he was clever enough to know were likely to happen in just those circumstances where witchcraft would be suspected; these are the circumstances that we are familiar with by now, when there has been a quarrel. Gifford also reminded his readers that the Devil would not be able to harm anyone unless God allowed it as a punishment, so that they would be wiser to search their consciences than go to a cunning man – as diviners were called in Elizabethan England – to have him find a witch. Gifford's wrath was greatest against the cunning men, who, he maintained, were also inspired by Satan and frequently accused the innocent. Logic did not require him to demonstrate that they were charlatans, however. He thought the 'subtlety' of the Devil extended to causing the remedies recommended by cunning men actually to work, but argued that to resort to them was no less witchcraft, and no less culpable, than the activities popularly ascribed to witches.

Speakers in the *Dialogue* say, as Africans have so often, 'A good riddance it were if the whole land could be set free from them', and 'I would they were all hanged up one against the other: we should not (I hope) stand in such fear of their spirits' (i.e. their familiars). The character who expresses Gifford's view, though he does not exonerate the witches, says, 'If there were no witches at all, yet men should be plagued by the devils in their bodies and souls', and, 'Shall we be so sottish as to think that [God] sendeth not the Devil now against ungodly men, to plague and to destroy them?' Gifford maintains that people evade the searching of conscience by ascribing to witches what is in fact deserved punishment, and that the 'cunning men' to whom they go for remedies are themselves sent by the Devil to distract them from attention to their sins and reliance on the scriptures for guidance: 'The faithful are to turn their eyes from the witch, and to deal with God, for from him the matter cometh'. Slightly modernised, this is just what a missionary might say to his congregation. The missionary might also be able to prescribe medical remedies, as Gifford's contemporaries could not to any great extent. But often his argument would fall on deaf ears as Gifford's did. The Devil, Gifford also argues, knows when people are going to die or fall ill from natural causes, and for his own glory stirs up some quarrel so that the sufferer may think he has been bewitched.

A much-quoted passage in the *Discourse* (with the spelling modernised) describes the sequence of events from quarrel to untoward event, from suspicion to accusation, just as an anthropologist today might observe them in Africa or elsewhere:

Some woman doth fall out bitterly with her neighbour; there followeth some great hurt . . . There is a suspicion conceived. Within few years after she is in jar with another. He is also plagued. This is noted of all. Great fame is spread of the matter. Mother *W* is a witch . . . Well, mother *W* doth begin to be very odious and terrible unto many, her neighbours dare say nothing but yet in their hearts they wish she were hanged. Shortly after another falleth sick and doth pine . . . The neighbours come to visit him. Well neighbour, saith one, do ye not suspect some naughty dealing; did ye never anger Mother *W*?'[3]

The man dies, denouncing Mother *W* in his last words, and she is condemned and hanged, protesting her innocence in *her* last words. All this in Gifford's view is contrived by the Devil to cause innocent people to suffer.

In the county of Essex, in south-eastern England, unusually full records extending over more than a century have been preserved, and these have recently been exhaustively examined by an historian, A. D. Macfarlane,[4] who combines the anthropologist's with the historian's approach. When the Essex trials are seen in perspective, as moments of crisis in small communities, generated by the quarrels between neighbours that come from the incidents of every day, the idea that they were nothing but a monstrously dramatic form of religious persecution becomes untenable; indeed it is Macfarlane's thesis that in Essex they were not a form of religous persecution at all. This is the only attempt that has so far been made to treat the belief in witchcraft at any period of European history as the kind of social reality with which we are familiar in African life.

We see, as in Africa, witchcraft as an explanation of misfortune. A different variety of misfortunes are referred to in anecdotes; we do not hear of ill-luck in hunting, which in seventeenth-century Essex was not part of the common man's mode of subsistence, but we hear of troubles with making butter and brewing beer, and a great deal about losses of livestock. Sickness is what makes people desperate, and death what makes them angry. Macfarlane remarks, however, that epidemics were not ascribed to witches, known or unknown, as they almost certainly would have been in Africa.

In Essex as in Africa there is a stereotyped picture of the witch. This does not ascribe to witches the sinister nocturnal activities and reversals of approved behaviour that are common to so many parts of the world: it merely says that witches are ugly, dirty and ill-natured old women. But, as in Africa, the bewitched person does not look for a witch who fits the stereotype, but for someone he has quarrelled with. A contrast with Africa is that the witches' familiars, which were small animals, were actually seen; and the appearance of a stray cat or ferret might be the first indication that witchcraft was afoot.

As in Africa, the diviner was often cautious and did not go beyond helping his client to focus suspicions. The client might offer the diviner names to choose from, or simply say 'Is it X. Y. ?' One of the most popular techniques in Essex was to make the client look in a mirror, where his imagination showed him the witch's face.

As in Africa, counter-magic was a possible means of defence, and this need not be obtained from specialists. It seems to have been common knowledge that if the butter would not churn the remedy was to stick a red hot horseshoe in it, and that if your animals were dying you had better burn one to death and this would put an end to the witchcraft. Both methods were supposed magically to burn the witch, though not to death; they merely frightened her off. As in Africa, again, one might move to another village out of reach of witchcraft; or refuse to let a suspected witch live near one, a measure that was easier in England with its freehold land ownership.

The causes of quarrels were such as arise every day among country neighbours; letting livestock stray on someone else's property, for example. Women – in England witches have nearly always been women – who begged and were refused were frequently believed to have taken revenge by witchcraft. One incident mentioned quite briefly by Macfarlane is so like the story of the old Ndembu woman who bewitched her young niece Ikubi to death that it deserves to be quoted. Nyamuwang'a, it will be remembered, passed by while Ikubi was cooking meat and asked for some. Ikubi said she only had enough for her own parents. In an Essex village Mother Cunny asked a neighbour for some drink, but his wife was busy with brewing, a more difficult process in England than it is in Africa, and said she had no time to get it. Next day the husband was ill.

Resemblances and differences are both interesting here. In both cases there is a good commonsense reason for the refusal. But in the African case both request and refusal are justified by an appeal to the norms of kinship. Young people ought to be generous to their elderly relatives, though if there is not enough to go round parents have priority over more distant kin, said Ikubi. In Essex the reason for refusal is purely technical – 'I can't leave my brewing'. The difference symbolises the difference between the African village, in which kinship is all-important, and the Essex village where neighbours are usually not kin, and Mother Cunny could only appeal to a neighbourly good-will which happened to be in abeyance at the moment.

Essex had its witch-finders, Matthew Hopkins and John Stearne, who have been execrated as charlatans, exploiting popular credulity at the cost of innocent lives, and as having been the instigators of the unusually large number of trials in 1645. Hopkins was originally perturbed by the amount of witchcraft he saw around his own home, and as he became well known he was invited to visit other villages, but it does not seem that he embarked on his career in response to a general feeling of panic. Unlike the African witch-finders who have been described, he could not have employed a simple automatic method of detection, since it was for the courts of law to decide who was guilty; he could only accuse, or prompt others to accuse by giving them new ideas about likely evidence. His speciality consisted in what might be called academic knowledge, such as had been elaborated on the continent and was discussed in the book by James vi and i, *Daemonologie*. The trials in which he was concerned were the first in England (though not in Scotland) to assume that persons guilty of witchcraft had made a compact with the Devil and attended the Sabbath with its obscene blasphemies. He also brought to Essex the 'swimming ordeal', the one element in witchcraft trials of which every layman has heard. Macfarlane's impression of Hopkins is that so far from being a conscious charlatan, he was concerned at what he sincerely believed to be the prevalence of evil and made it his vocation to root it out. He compares him with Bwanali.

Macfarlane's study is the first to show how much more closely the complex of behaviour surrounding the idea of witchcraft in seventeenth-century England resembles that in Africa than would be supposed if one looked only at the spectacular trials in which heretics are accused of witchcraft in the sense of diabolism. The Essex witches were not accused simply of *being* witches; before they could be indicted they had to be charged with some specific damage to a neighbour's person or property, and this was still so even after the advent of Matthew Hopkins.

But at the same time there are important differences. The African belief in witchcraft is part and parcel of the whole complex of religious ideas, on a level with the belief in punishment from the ancestors or the automatic disastrous results of breaking ritual restrictions. This complex can allow for the possibility that human volition may justifiably cause mystical harm as a punishment. The detection of witches is done by men who, though not priests, can certainly be thought of as having a religious function.

In Christian belief every event is the expression of God's purpose. This includes both good and ill fortune, and the latter may be sent not only as a punishment for sin, but also as a test of faith. In seventeenth-century Essex the reality of witchcraft is still taken for granted, but it is no longer one of several alternative explanations. If a person is bewitched, it must be because God allows it, but if he allows it this need not necessarily be as a punishment for some specific wrong-doing. Hence there is no such general inquest on behaviour as is often provoked by a case of sickness in Africa, and the attitude towards witches is much more like that of the Zande, or of the New Guinea peoples to sorcerers, simply an assumption that everyone is prone to do harm from malice. Hence too an attitude towards diviners that closely parallels, though for other reasons, that of European-made law in Africa. The diviner with his remedies and counter-measures is no longer an ally of religion; he is usurping the prerogative of God and tempting Christians to put their faith in human aid.

This picture shows Matthew Hopkins, the English witch-finder of Manningtree, Essex, who was active in 1645, and one of the women he accused, with the 'imps' or familiars whom she admitted to possessing. On the left is Sir John Holt, who as Chief Justice of England from 1691 set himself firmly against the conviction of witches. It should be noted that the last English execution took place in 1684, before he became Chief Justice.

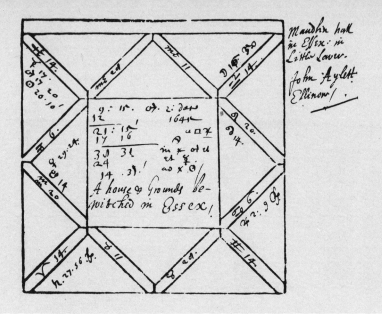

A house & Groundy bewitched in Essex

But sufferers seek human aid, and courses of action that are in their own hands, and therefore for a human cause of their afflictions: a person who may perhaps be induced to undo the harm and can at least be punished for it. No doubt the sick in seventeenth-century Essex prayed for relief as well, but the strongest faith was rarely enough. Macfarlane quotes from a pamphlet of the day the story of an Essex clergyman whose wife was dying and thought she knew the neighbour who had bewitched her. At first he reproved her for her want of faith and admonished her to trust God only, but finally he openly confronted the supposed witch and threatened, if his wife did not get better at once, not only to beat her up but have her hanged.

Yet another difference lies in the fact that from the sixteenth century onwards witchcraft in England was a crime defined by law, and tried in courts of law with formalised procedures. These courts had perforce to recognise that this particular crime could not be attested by witnesses as all others should, the very argument in Africa for recourse to divination and ordeals. In Africa in general,

A figure drawn by
a London astrologer in 1645
in order to calculate
the source of the witchcraft
afflicting his client

193

the divination may be said to *be* the trial, though punishment some-times rested with the decision of a political authority. In England the courts took no account of it; it was a private procedure for people who might want their suspicions confirmed before making an accusation or taking other action.

A manual of instructions to justices of the peace published in 1618 instructs them that in trials both for witchcraft and poisoning they may rely on 'half proofs' and take into account an accused person's antecedents and associates. People who might in other cases have been debarred from giving evidence were admitted here; spouses could testify against each other and children against their parents. The main criterion appealed to in Elizabethan days, how-ever, seems to have been the discovery on a person's body of marks or spots supposedly made by the Devil or the witch's familiar.

Three seventeenth-century clergymen, Perkins, Bernard and Gaule, wrote treatises which were intended to make judges more critical in the evidence they accepted, but nevertheless – inevitably as long as the reality of witchcraft was taken for granted – allowed them considerable latitude in relying on rumour and opinion. As their views are summarised by Macfarlane, they considered that there was a *prima facie* case if someone had a notorious reputa-tion as a witch; if somebody suffered damage after this person had cursed him or if she was even known to feel malice against him; if the victim recovered after counter-measures had been taken against the suspect; if she took a suspicious interest in the progress of the sickness; if she was kin or a close friend to a proven witch, or if she failed to pass the 'swimming' test. Since even today it is popularly supposed that people 'get their characteristics from' their parents there is nothing surprising in the notion of the inheritance of witch-craft; and daughters and granddaughters of witches appear to have been suspected rather oftener than they are in Africa. The 'swim-ming ordeal', which was not imposed in England before the seventeenth century, consisted actually in ducking the accused person, who was held by ropes. Those who were rejected by the water, and so could not sink – if there were any – were supposed to be witches; but those whom the ordeal showed to be innocent were not left to drown as is popularly supposed. A strong presumption of guilt was created by a death-bed confession of the victim or by an accusation from a cunning man. Accusation by another witch was conclusive evidence, as was the witch's mark, or the word of two witnesses who had seen the witch with her familiars, in this case often cats or dogs that anyone might possess. The many writers who have seen the witch trials of Europe as primarily a perversion of justice of which we should be ashamed would not regard this catalogue as a reason for modifying the severity of their judgment. But it shows at least that after the offence of witchcraft had been brought within the purview of the law there was an idea that some kind of principle should apply in dealing with it. It is not in itself evidence of a thirst for persecution.

But it does seem that another effect of the treatment of witchcraft as a statutory offence, in a society where the ruling class was literate, was to formalise and record a mass of free-floating folklore, so that the everyday witch, the cause of her neighbour's misfortunes, begins to merge with the witch of fantasy, and the trials begin to enquire into evil doings that are even more imaginary, if one may use the word in a comparative sense, than the causing of harm in circumstances where there may well have been ill-will.

The history of witchcraft trials on the continent, as far as we know it, bears this out. It is of course a reversal of chronology to treat English trials before those on the continent. My reason for doing so is that one, a well-documented, series of English trials has been examined by an historian whose initial presumption was that witchcraft is not necessarily to be identified with heresy, nor the trial of witches with religious persecution.

The earliest known (*circa* 1440) picture of witches flying on broomsticks, from *Le Champion des Dames* by Martin le Franc. Witches are everywhere believed to fly through the air at night, but outside Europe their steeds are generally nocturnal animals.

As far as seventeenth-century Essex is concerned Macfarlane has amply made his point. The records of other countries have not been studied from this point of view, and the standard works which treat of them are histories of persecution, focused on the question how people of great intellectual sophistication could have entertained beliefs that seem so irrational to the twentieth century, and have tortured and put to death numbers of people as a punishment for acts that they could not have committed. From the fifteenth century witchcraft acquires a new meaning. H. C. Lea, for instance, distinguishes witchcraft, in the sense of the pact with the Devil, from what he calls 'ordinary sorcery'. His massive volumes contain a few instances of the type with which the anthropologist is familiar, where somebody's cow goes dry and a neighbour is suspected, but they are concerned almost entirely with the spectacular trials at which the important evidence concerns participation in the Witches' Sabbath. The anthropologist would be inclined to assume that 'white witches' who offered to cure diseases had existed throughout the centuries, as indeed some do still, and that misfortunes had throughout the centuries been ascribed to the malice of neighbours, although we do not begin to hear about this until the point in time at which witchcraft came to be seen by those in authority as a form of heresy. But he would not be likely to agree that the suspicions and accusations of witchcraft between neighbours became any more prevalent because church and state were taking a new interest in it.

What did change was the attitude towards fantasies about the witches' nocturnal orgies and the imaginative embellishments of these. In the ninth century the official view was that the belief in witches itself was false, and that to hold it was to relapse into paganism. But with the appearance of heretical movements which rejected the authority of the church, the behaviour thought characteristic of witches began to be popularly attributed to heretics;

this happened long before church or state officially took cognisance of witchcraft. There was a long period of disputation over the possibility or otherwise of flying through the air and passing through keyholes, and here what is at least as interesting as the credulity of those who believed it possible is the attempt to find logical grounds for the belief. From an early stage in these discussions, too, there were men prepared to argue that the whole corpus of belief in the supernatural power of witches was illusory, and the indignation of the standard writers is largely directed against the obscurantism of those who would not listen to them.

To the relatively simple, and nearly universal, folk-lore of witches gathering at night to feast on their victims we find added in fifteenth-century Europe the new elaboration of the pact with the Devil making the witch his servant, and the Witches' Sabbath which is in essence a profanation of the Christian Mass. This was a new development in the Christian attitude towards witchcraft, displacing the older orthodoxy according to which the belief in the existence of witches was itself an illusion of the Devil. To square the new with the old it was argued that a 'new sect' of witches had appeared in the land, and it became a major aim of the Inquisition to root them out.

In this activity the Inquisition resembled the African witch-finders. In the opinion of Lea their insistence on the magnitude of the danger by itself stimulated the belief in witchcraft in the form of the compact with the Devil. In the light of the contemporary evidence from Africa and elsewhere an anthropologist would not suppose that fifteenth-century Europeans needed any prompting to ascribe their misfortunes to the ill-will of their neighbours or to suppose that men (or women) of ill-will abound. It may be that the association of these persons with the Witches' Sabbath made them seem more dreadful than their supposed malevolence by itself would have done, and so made those who conceived themselves to be victims or potential victims more determined on their destruction. It may well be that suspicions more readily crystallised into accusations because the inquisitors were anxious to hear them.

What differentiates western Europe and Scotland from England (most of the time) and Africa is the union of the real-life with the fantasy witch, the determination to secure confessions of dealings with the Devil and acts of devil-worship as well as of supposed injury to neighbours. One cannot conceive in Africa or New Guinea, or indeed among the Navaho, of a trial of people simply for *being* 'flying witches', as the trial of the Vaudois of Arras was.

The elaboration of the ideology of witchcraft goes with the development of a tradition of scholastic learning such as was only possible in a literate society, and of religious and political institutions seeking to make effective a centralised authority over an area much wider than was ever covered by any African polity. Literacy enabled the canon of orthodoxy to be established; communications better than those of Africa enabled it to be disseminated and enforced. The grafting of the Witches' Sabbath on the simpler folklore shows how far ingenious imaginations can go in picturing evil as the symbolic reversal of good. This too would not have been possible without the literacy and the organisation which established in detail an orthodox liturgy; and without a belief in a single God personifying all goodness it would not have been possible to conceive of a single Devil personifying all evil.

10 Theories of witchcraft

The theories that have been advanced in the discussion of witch-craft beliefs as they can be observed today are of different kinds. Some ask why such beliefs are so tenacious and so widely held. Some, considering beliefs and accusations together, ask what is their 'function' – that is to say, what do they *do* for the societies in which they are found? Do they contribute something indispensable to the maintenance of ordered social relations? Others seek to make correlations between different ways of directing accusations, or between the total number of accusations, or the proportion of mis-fortunes ascribed to witchcraft, and the structure of different societies.

The first type of theory is what is called functional. Such theories do not seek to show – as would be patently impossible – that societies of simple technology cannot do without the belief in witchcraft, but, at their largest, that it meets a necessity of social existence which must be met in one way or another, or, at their less ambitious, that, whatever its disadvantages, it makes some contri-bution to a socially desirable end.

Functional theories

Kluckhohn's theory of Navaho witchcraft is a functional one. As an American anthropologist with more interest in psychology than most British anthropologists have, he interprets witchcraft beliefs largely in terms of their significance for the individuals who hold them, in facilitating their adjustment to the society in which they have to live. 'Man craves reasons and explanations,' he writes, and these usually involve the personification of the agencies responsible for the events to be explained. This is, of course, the starting-point for Evans-Pritchard's justification of the belief in witchcraft as reasonable on its own terms, which every anthropologist now accepts. It enables people to put a name to their anxieties and feel they can take action to relieve them, again an interpretation common to all the writers quoted in this book. As Beattie would put it, it provides a 'stereotyped response' in situations of anxiety. But whereas Beattie and most social anthropologists are concerned with situations that society regards as giving cause for anxiety, Kluckhohn is discussing anxiety as a condition of individuals. He argues that Navaho believe in witchcraft not because they are consciously worried about specific circumstances, but because it canalises all the anxieties arising from 'generalised tensions produced by white pressure' as well as the frustrations that living in society imposes on us all. It provides for the displacement of aggression as well as of anxiety. People who would like to fight their parents or siblings, but are restrained by the rules of social behaviour, discharge their aggression on the imaginary person whom it is 'proper to fear and hate'. Few other means of expressing aggression are available to the Navaho, and without some means they would become a population of neurotics.[1] In the light of more detailed fieldwork one might say rather that the ascription of witchcraft permits hostile feelings against just those persons towards whom they would otherwise be forbidden.

This theory has been further developed by Marwick, also a psychologist, and also starting from the position that all persons experience tensions which must somehow be resolved. For Marwick, however, they are not resolved by deflecting hostile feelings from a dangerous to a harmless direction. Marwick's tensions are matters where conflict is recognised, and the means of resolution he mentions are judicial proceedings, the type of licensed rudeness between persons in specified relationships that anthropologists call 'joking', and accusations of witchcraft. The third is available for hostilities that are not amenable to the first procedure because they do not concern legal claims, or to the second because the enmity is not between parties to a 'joking relationship'. It would be generally

agreed that accusations of witchcraft arise out of breaches of moral obligations in which there is no claim that a chief's court could deal with. But Marwick would argue that *because* hostilities between members of one corporate body are denied an outlet in litigation the tension must be resolved through accusations of witchcraft.

Kluckhohn further argues that the belief in witchcraft reinforces confidence in magic for curing sickness, since its failures can be ascribed to the interference of witchcraft rather than its inherent inadequacy; that the image of the witch as capable of every forbidden act allows people to contemplate such acts with a clear conscience; and finally that it 'affirms solidarity by dramatically defining what is bad'.

Evans-Pritchard, who wrote earlier than Kluckhohn but was not quoted by him, makes more of the practical than the emotional value of witchcraft beliefs to those who hold them. He reminds us of something missionaries, doctors and anthropologists, from Livingstone to lesser men, have experienced when arguing against them, that our theories do not explain the selective incidence of disease or what we call accident. Whether we look to chance or providence for explanation, we have to admit that their workings are inscrutable.

Monica Wilson[3] was the first writer to show that witchcraft could not be discussed apart from religion – a view for which Mary Kingsley[4] had been rapped on the knuckles by Alfred Lyall a generation earlier. Her special interest was the religious beliefs of the Nyakyusa and the effect upon them of the work of Christian missions. At every turn she was brought up against the close connection between the mystical powers of good and evil – the chiefs' medicine of authority that in the wrong hands could destroy the kingdom, the alliance between the witches and the righteous when 'the breath of men' condemns a wrong-doer – and she saw witchcraft as one element in a complex of beliefs which interpret the world of man and nature as a moral order. This is not true of all societies that believe in the existence of witches. It does not appear to be true even of the Zande. But with the exception of the Zande it is characteristic of those African societies in which the belief in witchcraft and its consequences have been examined in detail.

Monica Wilson first discussed the stereotyped picture of the witch as the unneighbourly person, the one whom one would not wish to resemble, and also the one whom one should avoid offending, and showed how by both these ways of referring to witches the accepted code of behaviour was reinforced, particularly in talking to children. Lienhardt and Middleton developed the picture of the 'night-witch', the being nobody has ever seen, whose actions and associations represent everything that inspires disgust and fear, and also, in the case of the Lugbara, reversals of the normal that are not thought of as being in themselves obscene or immoral. Such a conception would seem to have a quite different significance from that of the unneighbourly person who may really one day be accused of witchcraft. It has the effect of asserting cultural values rather than specific social obligations. The real witch behaves badly in the accepted cultural context; the night-witch rejects culture altogether.

Generalisations about witches, then, assert by condemning their opposite the values of the society where the assertion is being made, and to this extent the belief makes its contribution to the maintenance of social order. But if we are looking for reasons why some societies cannot dispense with the belief in witchcraft, this might seem to be rather incidental, and of much less significance than their reliance on it as a recourse in misfortune.

Both these, however, are functional theories, and both, I would argue, are supported by the facts observed. The belief in witchcraft does offer a guide to action when disaster strikes, albeit a misleading one; it enables people to imagine that they are taking the right steps to remedy it. It does hold up to the members of most societies which accept it an image of what they should not be. No anthropologist disputes this.

There is, however, another functional explanation which is less widely accepted. This is that the belief in witchcraft enables people to break off relationships that have become intolerable, but that could not be rejected unless one party to the relationship were held to be guilty of the most heinous of possible offences. This theory is built on examples of lineage fission such as those that were recounted in detail in chapter 6. It will be easier to discuss after some consideration of the theories that link the practical expression of the belief in witchcraft with the structure of different societies.

The direction of accusations

A cliché of British anthropology is 'Witchcraft accusations are not random'. This might well provoke the retort, 'Of course they are not, since we know that the victims of misfortune hold their enemies responsible'. What it really means was expressed by Kluckhohn when he said the incidence of accusations in a population was not random. He went on to mention categories of persons held by the Navaho to be likely witches, but did not in fact deal with accusation as opposed to suspicion.

British anthropologists have given much attention to the question whether persons in some particular social relationship are especially apt to accuse one another of witchcraft. Thus Nadel[5] observed among the Mesakin of the Nuba hills in Kordofan that nearly all accusations of witchcraft were made against men who were thought to have caused the death of their sisters' sons. He associated this with the fact that in this matrilineal society the senior man is expected to give a cow to his nephew when the latter reaches puberty. This is a recognition of adulthood; it is the young man's first share of the herd that he will one day inherit. The older men dislike having to make this gift, which they see as the first sign that authority must pass from them, and sometimes refuse it when they are asked. This is the only recorded instance of witchcraft ascribed to someone's resentment against a person whom he has wronged, and even if Nadel intended to convey that the importunity of the younger men had annoyed the elder it would still be an unusual explanation. One wonders whether, if he had lived longer among the Mesakin, he would have found that these accusations were associated with other grounds for hostility.

Godfrey Lienhardt[6] has discussed the direction of accusations among the Dinka of the southern Sudan. He did not find there that persons in authority were believed to bewitch their subordinates or vice versa. The only accusation that he actually heard anyone make was in a quarrel between two wives of one man, and even this was little more than an exchange of insults leading to a brawl. The injury in question here was the failure of one woman's millet garden, a misfortune that is commonly ascribed to the jealousy of co-wives in polygynous societies. It is not the kind of injury that would of itself lead to a serious accusation; rather it would be a stage in the development of a mutual dislike which would eventually be held to account for some sickness (including a woman's barrenness) or death. Dinka offered as examples of people who might accuse one another the wives of one man, the sons of the same father and different mothers, or a woman and her brother's wife. Lienhardt observes that in all these relationships there are elements of conflict, but the parties cannot avoid one another and so cannot well express open hostility. Yet they are not persons whose relative status is clearly defined so that the inferior is not permitted to find fault with the behaviour of the superior. He adds that in all cases the parties to conflict are linked through being associated with some one man, but does not develop this point.

In every polygynous society where property passes from father to son, co-wives and their respective children are in competition for the affections of the common husband or father and for the resources which he controls. The reason for conflict between sisters-in-law is not so clear, and is not discussed by Lienhardt. Gluckman[7] offers an explanation of another kind, based on the social structure of the Zulu homestead. Here, it may be noted, co-wives accuse one another despite the fact that they are formally ranked in order of marriage. Gluckman's view rests on a well-recognised attitude towards the women who are brought in as wives to an extended family consisting of a father with his married sons, or possibly of brothers with their sons. As the component families of such a group develop there is bound to be rivalry for their share of the common resources, and this leads sooner or later to a division of the property and the break-up of the group. But the ideal is that not only should sons remain with their fathers, as they commonly do, but brothers should keep together, and the men of the homestead are unwilling to blame themselves when this becomes impossible. Just the same thing happens with the Indian joint family, though there divisions are blamed simply on the quarrelsomeness of the wives. The Zulu, because they explain misfortunes by resentment growing out of quarrels and expressed in witchcraft, make the women, the outsiders to the lineage, responsible for the quarrelling and so also hold them responsible for the misfortunes.

This still does not account for accusations made against sisters-in-law. Gluckman suggests another explanation here. He reminds us that, although a woman is a member of her father's lineage along with her brothers, lineage property does not pass through her to her children, and that for this reason there is in some societies 'a kind of ritual antipathy between a man and his sister'. The implication is that the sister resents the fact that she cannot transmit lineage property to her children, and that this is formally recognised in the 'ritual antipathy'. This, Gluckman says, 'may be the clue to why sisters of the patrilineage accuse its wives of witchcraft'. However, he does not pursue the clue; this must be left for later students, and if a convincing solution is to be found, I suggest that it will have to be done by the kind of careful tracing of relationships over a period of time that characterises the work of Middleton and Turner. At present we have not many case-histories to illustrate this theme.

It must be remembered that we are dealing with small settlements or villages in which inter-relationships are defined, and expectations of correct behaviour formed, in terms of the obligations of kinship and affinity. When one writes of a difficult relationship one means something much more constraining than the

Apparatus of a doctor-diviner in Sierra Leone. Note that the collection includes imported objects. The possession of medicine-bottles is often taken as evidence of the practice of sorcery.

difficult relationship of friends who do not wish to part or of colleagues at work. The villager is committed to his membership of a kin group and to his links with the kin of his affines. Only one of his relationships, that of marriage, is freely chosen, and sometimes not that. This is what the anthropologists have in mind who say that witchcraft is characteristic of small-scale societies. It is obvious that the belief is not, and that accusations of witchcraft are not confined to very small societies. But it is no accident that the richest accounts of the ways in which people simultaneously express hostility and try to remedy their misfortunes by accusations of witchcraft come from villages that are very small by African standards. Nor, perhaps, is it accidental that Evans-Pritchard did not find a particular 'pattern' of accusations among the Zande. The descriptions of lineage fission that I have quoted come from peoples with a minimum of political organisation, 'tribes without rulers', as they have been called. In these societies the accusation of witchcraft is a form of political competition, and a close study of a village or settlement where such accusations are bandied about shows clearly how they are directed in this way. Of course I do not mean by this that people make accusations that they do not believe to be true in order to further their ambitions; they do believe that witches are at work, and they naturally suppose that the witches must be the people who have reason to be opposed to their interests. In a village of Zande commoners, where there can be no political competition because they are all subjects of a single royal family, one would expect the quarrels that lead to accusation of witchcraft to be matters simply of actions held to run counter to the norms of kinship and neighbourliness, and not to divide villages into factions; and one would expect rivalries between princes to be decided by the strength of the following that they can mass for a contest of arms, and not by accusations of secret evil. One cannot say, however, that in *every* society without centralised political organisation competition for power is carried on by accusations of witchcraft.

Middleton's *Lugbara Religion* gives the only detailed account that we have in which suspicions of witchcraft are associated with the division of a lineage; yet we know that lineage division is a regular feature of patrilineal as of matrilineal societies. It is not only from the Ndembu, but also from many other peoples of the 'matrilineal belt' that stretches across Africa from the Congo to Zambia and Malawi, that we hear most of accusations of witchcraft in connection with the division of villages, and it seems that this fact must be connected in some way with the very unstable nature of village populations in this area, itself to be correlated with the matrilineal mode of reckoning descent.

Any society which reckons descent through the mother has to come to terms with the fact that the father is the head of the domestic family although he is an outsider to his childrens' lineage; hence a conflict between a man's attachment to his family and to his lineage is built into the system. In the simplest terms, the alternatives are that men grow to adulthood either in their mother's lineage home, to which their father is an outsider, or in their father's, to which they are outsiders themselves. The Ndembu rule is the latter: the women of the lineage leave home when they marry – unless they marry sons of men of their own lineage who have grown up in the village. Every woman hopes eventually to return to her lineage home, and so do her sons; but since they have grown up outside the village, they have not the same closeness to their cousins as one finds in a patrilineal settlement, where the sons of all the brothers have known one another from childhood. There is no claim to land that would hold people to one locality rather than another; the most important heritable asset is the office of headman. Ambitious men compete for this office, using, among other means, accusations of witchcraft against their rivals, but those who fail, and also those who see they have no chance, secede and found their own villages, often making the suspicion of witchcraft their reason for moving.

At this point two types of theoretical explanation merge: that which looks for characteristic 'patterns' of accusation and explains them by the 'tensions' in particular social relationships, and the form of functional theory which sees accusations of witchcraft as socially valuable because they 'relieve tensions'. The latter has been called the 'cathartic' theory, and where accusations have been associated with the division of a social group, it has also been described by the word 'obstetric'.

Kluckhohn's interpretation of the belief in witchcraft as a means of relieving tension was entirely different from the Africanists'.

After enumerating the various familial relationships that give rise to tension he argued that this tension was relieved by expressing hatred against 'totally unrelated' persons. In fact he attached little importance to the connection between witchcraft and specific causes for resentment. The Africanists, on the other hand, see the 'cathartic' effect of the belief in witchcraft in that it allows people to express the hostilities that they ought not to feel, and are only justified in feeling if they can believe that they are suffering through someone else's unjustified hostility.

The 'cathartic' effect of witchcraft is sometimes described in general terms in the statement that an accusation of witchcraft – which of course could not be made unless there was a belief in witchcraft – can justify the expression of hostility in relationships which are supposed to imply mutual affection, and so make possible the ending of an intolerable relationship. Societies that believe in witchcraft are not of course the only ones where it is held that people should put up with more from their kin than from other people, and need stronger grounds for breaking contact with them than they would for letting a friendship lapse; these grounds would usually be some failure to observe the norms of kinship. It is where misfortunes are assigned to personified causes that witchcraft provides them.

Much more has been made, however, of the 'cathartic function' in connection with the division of villages. Marwick wrote, in relation to the Cewa:

Witch beliefs and accusations of witchcraft serve to blast down dilapidated parts of the social structure and clear the rubble in preparation for the development of new ones . . . The air-clearing storms of Cewa witchcraft accusation permit periodic redistributions of structural forces and by this means maintain the virility of the indigenous social structure.[8]

Stripped of metaphor, what does this mean? If anything is

dilapidated, it is the corporate solidarity of one section of the descendants of a common ancestor; a state of mind rather than an element of social structure. There is really very little to blast down and clear away; a social structure based on genealogical descent renews itself automatically. Mary Douglas[9] has criticised this argument on the ground that when the poison ordeal was freely used the wrong men might have been convicted, and the secessionist younger generation would then have been denied the opportunity to found their new village elsewhere. She argues further that the large size – for Central Africa – of Cewa villages indicates that in fact Cewa villages divide less frequently than others; hence it is possible that heads of lineages actually keep revolt in check by successfully accusing their juniors. It is also possible, however, that other factors make membership of a large lineage attractive, so that the desire to secede does not develop as frequently as it does among the Ndembu. If this were so one would expect that there might be long periods during which, as happened once among the Ndembu even in the dramatic time when Turner was there, accusations would turn on petty quarrels between persons of little significance to even these minuscule struggles for power.

The question why contention between lineages is characteristically expressed through witchcraft accusations among these matrilineal peoples is an interesting one, but it cannot be given a functional answer in the sense that they 'have to' believe in witchcraft in order that the village can divide when the time is ripe for this. My own view would be that the functional explanation is valid only in connection with the ascription of misfortune to witchcraft; people do 'have to' have an explanation of their misfortunes.

Mary Douglas has carried furthest the attempt to relate different ideas and behaviour concerning witchcraft to the structure of the societies where they have been studied. She begins by asking how the importance of witchcraft as an explanation of misfortune varies. This is something difficult to measure quantitatively. Marwick[10] sought to make such a calculation, taking 194 'cases of misfortune', some in the villages where he was living and others told to him by informants whom he asked to search their memory. He found that fifty-five per cent of the total were ascribed to sorcery. It was also interesting that twenty-five per cent, most of them deaths, were held to be 'acts of god'; this might be taken to confirm the view that at times when feelings within a community are not inflamed, sorcery is not invoked as a reason for deaths unless there is something unexpected about them.

Mary Douglas lists six Central African peoples in order of the frequency of village fission, judged in part at least by the size of villages. For each people she notes how far accusations of witch-craft are invoked in contests for authority, whether or not witch-craft is the dominant explanation of misfortune, what is the range of persons between whom accusations are made, and what cate-gories of person are typically accused. One of the results of this collection of data is to show that accusations are sometimes brought against persons in authority, sometimes against the subversive, sometimes equally against both, while among the least organised people of all, the Plateau Tonga, accusations 'fall randomly on persons in conflict'. This last is perhaps the most significant state-ment, since it admits that, where there is no political competition, or political struggles are conducted by other means, there will still be quarrels, and as long as misfortunes are thought to be caused by ill-feeling there will be accusations of witchcraft. Mary Douglas asserts that the ideas of the Plateau Tonga on mystical causation are 'not strongly dominated by witchcraft/sorcery beliefs'. Never-theless, they use diviners and witch-finders as their neighbours do.

In her conclusion, in which she refers to the Zande, by contrast a very highly organised society, she repeats Lienhardt's theory that accusations are exchanged between persons whose relative status

is not rigidly defined – as she puts it, 'in the cracks and crevices of the social system'. She adds, 'in very small-scale, face-to-face situations'. I should consider this qualification superfluous, since people can only quarrel face-to-face.

An interesting further development of the theme, however, is the explanation offered for the restriction of accusations to women. Here Mary Douglas follows Gluckman's argument that political rivalry in some societies is expressed by accusing some woman of the rival lineage who is married to a member of the accuser's group, and so is an outsider in his homestead. As she ingeniously puts it, 'tensions between men are dealt with as if they were only tensions between women'.

One does seem to find in these theories rather too much suggestion that somebody – in this case it would seem the men of a society – deliberately makes rules about who is to be accused. Mary Douglas writes about 'kinds of social limitation placed on accusations' and of 'witch-beliefs so limited and controlled that they do not disrupt those relations between men which constitute the formal structure of the social system'.

We seem to be invited to imagine people who would like to accuse *X* but are somehow constrained instead to accuse *Y*. But we must return to the association of witchcraft with quarrels. In hierarchically organised societies, societies resting, as Jacques Maquet put it, on 'the premise of inequality', there are relationships in which people *cannot* quarrel; the subordinate can only resent. One might ask why this kind of resentment should not be expressed in witchcraft, and there one might find the answer in the belief, which in Africa at least is general, that witchcraft arises out of quarrels between people who *ought to be friends;* persons of different social rank are not expected to be friends.

However satisfactory this explanation might be for Africa, it does not take into account the one analysis of the direction of witchcraft accusations that has been made in a non-African context, Macfarlane's study of Essex in the seventeenth century. He did not there find that accusations were made between kin, and this is what one would expect where the system of land tenure did not constrain kin to live together, and geographical mobility was greater than in most parts of Africa. But he did find a 'pattern'. That is, the people accused of witchcraft were not merely (if they were at all) eccentric old crones persecuted because they were defenceless, but women who had begged or sought favours from the more substantial persons in the village, had been refused and then supposedly revenged themselves by witchcraft. Here again we see the issue of failure in a moral obligation, or of the interpretation of this obligation to the disadvantage of the supposed witch. Macfarlane sees the accusations as inspired by guilty conscience, a view that interestingly parallels the idea of some African societies that the mystical agencies of deserved punishment call the witches to their aid. He explains the decline in prosecutions in England by the move away from the idea of charity as a general Christian duty to the idea that it should not be given indiscriminately, paralleled by the development of formal institutions for the relief of the poor.

This is certainly a more convincing explanation of the decline of trials for witchcraft in England than that offered by Gluckman,[11] who not only correlates this with the industrial revolution but tells us that when that historical process got under way 'accusations of witchcraft were ruled illegal'. Gluckman is here concerned with the African belief that people who are more prosperous than the average must have had recourse to sorcery – a belief that of itself does not lead to accusation – and appears to hold that English society up to the industrial revolution was as egalitarian as the Ndembu or Nyakyusa, and therefore much more egalitarian than the Nupe or Nyoro. But what is startling in the writing of a lawyer is to find the removal of witchcraft from the statute book described as if it had been a measure like the Witchcraft Suppression Ordinances enacted in Africa. Actually the last witch trial, in 1717, preceded the repeal of the British witchcraft laws by twenty years, and the English Peasants' Revolt preceded this event by more than three centuries.

It is possible that studies focused on the tracing of the direction of accusations and correlating this with different types of social structure have gone as far as they can usefully go. Since it is the primary task of a social anthropologist to elucidate the structure of relationships between members of the society he is studying, there is something a little paradoxical in the idea that he must count up accusations of witchcraft so as to find out which relationships are most likely to be sources of conflict. This was first done before we had seen so clearly the close connection between accusations of witchcraft and recent quarrels; and, in so far as the generalisations made reported the generalisations of Africans and not the anthropologists' observations, they threw new light on the way the informants thought of their own society. But now that we have this information, we can surely *begin* by looking at relationships which are likely to be sources of conflict. We already have a good idea, at any rate for Africa, of the main types of kinship system, and we do not find that what we are told about accusations of witchcraft reveals striking differences within these types.

The approach advocated by Turner is to look at the whole field of factors affecting the exchange of accusations, and see, as he saw in his story of Mukanza village, how the direction of accusations, the treatment of the accused person and indeed the very question whether an attempt should be made to identify a witch, depend on the balance within this total field at any given time. One might then find, for example, not simply that 'mothers' brothers' are wont to accuse 'their sisters' sons', but rather that a man is accused by one of his mother's brothers while the rest are seeking to defend him and pin the guilt on somebody else; and if this is so, it will be because of some factional division in the small community and not because of some intrinsic 'tension' in the relationship between every man and his sisters' children. In fact, one may reduce a good deal of the mystique of theories about witchcraft to one or two commonsense observations. The statement 'Witchcraft cannot operate at a distance' can be translated into 'People cannot quarrel unless they are in contact'. It is not so easy to translate 'Witchcraft only operates within the lineage', but one might doubt whether on close examination this statement would anywhere prove to be true; if it did, one would relate it to the well-known fraternal enmity which is often connected with claims on a common patrimony. People do quarrel when they ought to be friends; people do continue to feel resentment when they should not. If people assume that these feelings can actually injure the objects of them – and this is the assumption that I have suggested is functionally necessary in their state of technical knowledge – then all we have to do is to look out for quarrels. Nobody, as far as I know, has suggested that it is a profitable occupation to look for types of quarrel and correlate them with different social systems. I hold to this commonsense view even if it be said – as it has been said – that 'it doesn't take an anthropologist to say that'.

Some writers have sought to correlate the prevalence of accusations of witchcraft with the absence of judicial institutions. Those who correlate them with the absence of formal political institutions might be nearer the mark, as I have suggested in comparing the circumstances in which they can or cannot be used in the competition for authority. The Dinka, who have no judicial organisation, appear in practice to make accusations much less often than the Zulu, among whom a hierarchy of territorial chiefs hold courts, and it seems that the same type of accusation is liable to be made in both societies. Some chief's courts hear accusations of sorcery; a large collection of records of such cases from the Tswana has been made by Schapera. A number of the Rhodesian cases cited by Crawford were discussed in the courts of kraal heads or chiefs. Decisions about the treatment of witches were taken by Zande princes and Nyakyusa chiefs. And what about Europe?

Quarrels and grudges

Accusations of witchcraft, in fact, cannot be regarded as alternatives to challenges before judicial authorities. They are concerned with different kinds of dispute – with disputes which could not of themselves give rise to legal action because they are not about matters of jural rights. Much has been made of the fact that witchcraft is conceived as an act of secret hostility between people who ought to be friendly. But the ideal of friendliness is itself the essence of a relationship that rests on moral and not legal bonds. The people who *ought* to be friendly are those who *ought* to share their resources, who have a joint patrimony and in their relationship to the rest of society are an indivisible jural unit. Obligations between the members of such units cannot be strictly defined, and those who control resources – even so small a resource as a little meat in the cooking-pot – often have to weigh one against another.

The *Glé*. This model of a monstrous head is imported by the Niaboua of the Ivory Coast from the Kissi who themselves got it from Liberia. To divine by it a man places it on the head of his wife or child, who answers the questions put to it, supposedly as its medium.

219

The nature of the quarrels which give rise to accusations of witchcraft, then, makes it impossible to imagine a person choosing between recourse to law and making an accusation. But what makes this even more impossible is the very nature of the situations in which the belief in witchcraft is invoked. Witchcraft may be *threatened* in a quarrel, and it seems that people engaged in quarrels frequently use those sinister expressions, 'You will see [something you won't like]' or 'You *may* [or may not] sleep well'. But it cannot be *suspected* until it has borne fruit. In other words, there must be a misfortune before there can be a reference to witchcraft, and when the accusation is made it is the aggrieved person, not the one who has caused the grievance, who is held to be at fault. The offence now is not the rejection of a claim but the harbouring of a grievance.

The African association of witchcraft with concealed grudges reflects the high value set in a small community on peaceful relationships which are more than the absence of open hostility. It reflects also the fear of the hidden enemy that is to be found in most societies, and that some would see as the very source of the idea of the witch. Obviously village relationships would be no easier if people paraded their grudges, but the ideal is that those who feel them should admit them openly and then forget them – not, of course, without an admission of error from the person who caused the grudge. The Tallensi express this idea in their belief that the annual rituals to secure prosperity will be 'spoiled' if those who attend them have unreconciled quarrels; in this case there is no question of witchcraft or deliberate malice, simply a disturbance of the moral order. It will be remembered that one of the symbolic objects in the Ndembu diviner's basket represents 'the grudge', and that an important part of his technique consists in seeing what other symbols lie close to it in the basket. Ndembu, in this respect resembling some other African peoples, believe that God, or the relevant spirits, may send a sickness as a merited punishment for quarrelling among kin. For the ritual treatment of such sickness, it is considered essential for all persons who have grudges against one another or against the patient to confess them.

Associated with this is the idea that a witch who has caused a misfortune short of death can be persuaded to undo it by an expression of goodwill to the sufferer. With the Zande, exceptionally, this does not appear to imply a discussion of grievances or even an admission of responsibility; the Zande evade this by recourse to the theory that witchcraft is involuntary. It must be rare, moreover, for someone who is challenged as a witch to admit the charge, and, as many of the examples show, the grievance of the supposed witch is often known to the accusers, and is indeed the ground for the accusation.

But in this context the witch may be contrasted not merely with the ideal member of society, who, when he thinks someone has done him an injury, confronts him openly, gets satisfaction and forgets the whole matter, but also with those who, with right on their side, express their indignation by making the offender ill – the Nyakyusa villagers with their whispers of disapproval, the Lugbara elder and his counterpart in other societies with their invocation of the spirits. It is not guilt that they admit to, merely responsibility for action taken in support of accepted standards – though they too could not make any admission until some sickness showed them that their action had been effective.

It may be that some at any rate of the confessions of witchcraft that are recorded from African societies are motivated by ideas of this kind. Both Evans-Pritchard and Denise Paulme have remarked, in the context of widely separated societies, that nobody can be sure he is not a witch. This may well be the reflection, not so much of theories of Zande type that witchcraft is actually a substance which operates without the knowledge of its possessor, as of a generalised notion that anger and hatred can of themselves cause harm to others. The confessions of specific impossible acts recorded by Crawford are very different from those that M. J. Field heard at the Ghanaian spirit shrines. We do not know the context of any of them in the sense of the supposed witch's past history and relations with her neighbours. But where people, without describing what they say they have done, simply avow responsibility for deaths in their neighbourhood, one must bear in mind that they live in a world where nobody challenges the possibility of causing death by witchcraft. They themselves would suspect others in appropriate circumstances. They may or may not have known they were suspected and begun to wonder 'Perhaps it *was* my doing'. Possibly, as Field suggests, their psychological state may have moved them to this without any prompting.

11 Witchcraft in the Christian context

When we turn from the writings of anthropologists to the classic studies of witchcraft in Europe we find ourselves in another world. To one who approaches them by way of Africa the difference in the treatment of the subject is at first inexplicable. Then one realises that for the writers on the 'witch-craze' of the fifteenth to seventeenth centuries witches are the supposed members of the 'new sect' that, according to the inquisitors, appeared in Europe some time after 1400. A witch is now defined as a person who has made a compact with the Devil and attends the Witches' Sabbath in order to worship him, to profane Christian ritual, to feast on the bodies of children and indulge in obscene orgies. As servants of the Devil, witches are believed to be capable of producing all the many types of misfortune that can be assigned to no other cause, but these are now significant as evidence of association with the Devil rather than as offences in themselves.

The questions that have been asked by writers about Europe concern the reason why people should have believed in the compact with the Devil and why those accused should have been tortured to make them confess to it. They do not ask why misfortunes were supposed to be caused by witches; this is left to *The Golden Bough* and taken for granted as the superstition of the times. They are more interested in the activities of lawyers and churchmen seeking to root out heresy than in what ordinary people did when they thought they were bewitched. Hence the major works are studies of witch-finding rather than of witchcraft. They ask the legitimate question why this should be pursued more actively at one time than another, but they are concerned rather with the direction of witch-finding from above than with popular demand for the services of witch-finders. Hence it is not easy to answer the question in terms of the kind of local calamity which might have stimulated a purge of witches in Africa.

Here and there one finds little details that illustrate the kind of situation we are familiar with in Africa. Late frosts or an unduly long winter are ascribed to witches in two cases a century apart, quoted by the great American scholar Lea in his *History of the Inquisition*.[1] He also tells a story that could equally well have come from contemporary Africa or seventeenth-century Essex, of a man whose cattle were dying, and who said he suspected a woman who was a reputed sorceress. She said to his wife, 'Your husband has done ill in saying that I killed his cattle, and he will find it so before long'. And next night this woman fell grievously ill, but she recovered when her husband went and threatened the witch. Julio Caro Baroja, commenting on another recorded trial, writes, 'The bitterness of family feuds often makes itself clearly felt in the evidence taken down by the clerks'.[2]

European witch-finders, like African ones, believed in automatic tests of witchcraft, but the African tests rested solely on the authority of the witch-finder. This might be supported by belief in his medical powers, notably that of removing from a sick person's body objects supposed to have been put there by witchcraft, but he was not required to give reasons for his use of a particular test; this was just a part of his total mystical insight. Certain European bishops claimed to be able to recognise a witch at sight, but they were exceptional.

Fifteenth-century Europe, with its long tradition of disquisition and argumentation, its preservation in writing of the views of earlier generations, its love for systematisation and its concern with what it was permissible for a Christian to believe, developed a new pseudo-science of demonology, based in part on supposed instances of bewitching, in part on the universal fantasy of the night-witch, and in part on the elaboration of this fantasy which makes it the obscene counterpart of the Christian Mass. In this context rules for the detection of witches are linked with the natural history of witchcraft, if it may be so called: witches do not sink in water because the pure element, used in the sacrament of baptism, rejects them; witches have marks on their bodies where the Devil stamped them when they gave him their allegiance; witches have nipples in strange parts of their bodies, through which they suckle their familiars. The possibility that witchcraft may be stronger than counter-magic, and so impair the judgment of divination or ordeal, appears in the sophisticated form of the idea that the Devil may confer on his subjects a gift of taciturnity which enables them to refuse confession even under torture. But this influence may again be countered by recourse to objects associated with Christian ritual, and the Devil's power is held to be in abeyance on Christian holy days. Or the Devil's own aid could be invoked by calling in other magicians; the ethics of such a procedure was the kind of question that was earnestly discussed. There was argument whether a person named by an accused witch as having been present at the Sabbath could be charged on this evidence alone; suppose the Devil had created apparitions so as to get innocent people into trouble? Some said that without this evidence witches would never be discovered; others that it was not sufficient without additional 'conjectures and presumptions'.

The classic writers on European witchcraft are interested only a little in the question what events led to the prosecution of witches in specific places at particular moments, and much more in the nature of the dialogue between those who believed in all the enormities of which witches were accused, those who argued that some at least were impossible, and those who rejected the whole complex of beliefs. Lea sometimes writes as if nobody would have ascribed misfortunes to witchcraft had not the church been assiduously teaching people to do so. But he is right in remarking that the notion of the compact with the Devil was raised by the church from the status of fairy-tale to that of reality. In the first place this was an illustration of the miraculous powers of the Virgin.

There was a story current from about the ninth century of a priest who sold his soul to the Devil in return for honour and riches in this life, but then repented and prayed to the Virgin, who saved him by taking from the Devil the document he had signed and giving it back to him. In the eleventh and twelfth centuries this was a favourite theme of sermons, and certainly familiarised the general public with this early version of the Faust legend. The witch trials do not have much to say about its glamorous aspect – the satisfaction of every desire up to the moment when the Devil claims his payment and carries the soul to hell. But in a general atmosphere of belief in magic and in the Devil as a person there is no reason why people should not believe this was possible; and Lea, here following the same line as the French nineteenth-century historian Michelet, thinks it very probable that downtrodden peasants might have thought they had more to hope from a pact with him than from obedience to a God who seemed to have abandoned them. Some may even have thought they had made such a pact.

But this does not account for the denunciations of others whom the accused witches were supposed to have seen at the diabolic feasts. The commonsense view is that people were obliged under torture to give names of some kind; that some of the names may have been of enemies of the accused; that sometimes they may have known whom the judges wished to see inculpated. A striking fact of some continental trials was that accused persons would sometimes name others who lived a long way away. Thus the most famous trial in Flanders, that of the Vaudois of Arras in 1460, was set in motion by the accusations of a man of Langres who was burned as a witch, and at the Arras trials people in Amiens and Tournay were named. This, as much as the idea of panic, is what led Lea to use the metaphor of the 'infection' of witchcraft.

Witchcraft as a pre-Christian religion ?

One theory which has had some popular currency is that there really *was* a Witches' Sabbath, though it should not have been called by that name. This was the view of the Egyptologist Margaret Murray.[3] Her argument is based in part on writings of the period of the great witch trials, those of such sceptics as Reginald Scot in England as well as the works of Bodin and De Lancre, French jurists who were convinced of the reality of the practices they were seeking to root out. She also relied on statements made in confessions, in particular those of the North Berwick witches who were accused of conspiracy against James vi (later James i of England). In her interpretation what she calls the witch-cult was in fact the pre-Christian religion of Britain and western Europe, kept alive by faithful adherents who maintained their faith under torture, just as Christian martyrs did in other circumstances. The Devil whom so many said they had seen was an actual man, a priest to whom acts of worship were performed because a god was thought to be incarnate in him. The cult had its solemn ritual, in which the swearing of allegiance and rejection of the rival religion had a logical part. The stories of the appearance of the Devil in animal form describe rituals in which the priest wears an animal mask, though many of the descriptions given by accused witches of the Devil in animal form refer to other than ritual occasions. The 'Devil's marks' were made by tattooing. The name Sabbath was not given, as most writers suppose, as an offensive reference to Jewish practices; it came from *s'ébattre*, to be gay. The faithful did not really fly through the air to go to it; most of the members of any local section lived within walking distance of the meeting-place. There were general gatherings for ritual at fixed times and special meetings for the purpose of making charms; some of these were fertility charms (even though the witches whose testimony is

The opening bars of the last movement
('Witches' Sabbath') of Berlioz' *Fantastic Symphony*
(1830). Autograph MS, Bibliothèque Nationale, Paris.
It is not only artists and writers who have
taken up the theme of witchcraft and its orgies.

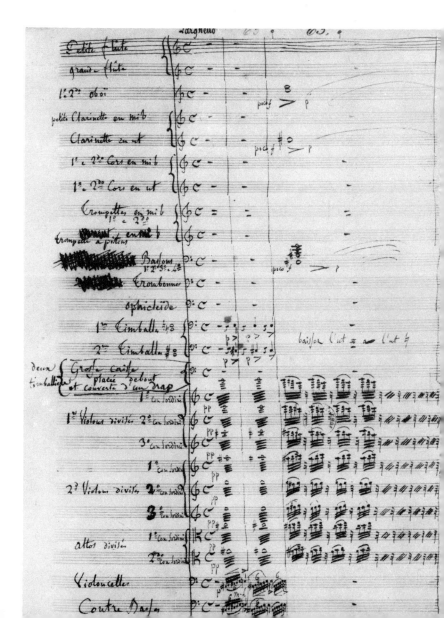

quoted may not have realised that this was their purpose), but many were for making harmful spells; some of these are specifically referred to in confessions. In this religion there were a number of Devils, one for each coven or congregation, who is equated with the 'master of the coven'. This man might organise some of the faithful to produce by physical means the results attributed to the spells (destruction of crops, or even on one occasion of a bridge), in order to maintain his prestige with the less sophisticated. Even the kissing under the tail of the Devil in animal form is given the explanation that under the tail of the masked figure was a face that worshippers were required to kiss.

The manner of Margaret Murray's exposition, which would be appropriate to the statement of uncontested facts, might well lead unwary readers to take it as authoritative, and no doubt accounts to some extent for the prestige that her book has had. But careful study might raise some doubt in the mind even of the general reader. Her treatment of the records is distinctly arbitrary. Sometimes they are taken as simple statements of fact, at other times it seems that the witches did not understand the experiences they were recalling, for example the purpose of the charms they helped to make. When they were tattooed they could not describe this more precisely than by talking of 'pricking', 'nipping', or 'a mark with an iron awl' (*une aleine de fer*). When it suits the theory we are to believe in the murder of children as a sacrifice for fertility, but the eating of children's flesh is 'probably an exaggeration'.

In fact Margaret Murray invented a religion for the purposes of her argument, and she saw nothing strange in a congregation which held business meetings – her chosen phrase – to discuss means of harming specific persons. It did not seem to her necessary to explain why their beliefs should be held to entitle them to take such action; if she thinks the bewitchings were reprisals against persecutors of the supposed religion, she does not say so. The religion she describes does not in fact have a morality; it simply consists (apart from the business meetings for the purpose of witchcraft in the more commonly accepted sense of the word) of rites for the promotion of fertility.

Now it can be argued that there are religions concerned entirely with rituals to achieve the desires of the worshippers, and not at all with rules of conduct between man and man. But these are just the religions in which little importance is attached to witchcraft. To an anthropologist with witch beliefs outside Europe in mind, the real weakness of Margaret Murray's theory is that if witches were merely the adherents of a religion as this is ordinarily understood *there would be no witches*. In the rest of the world witches are by definition those who reject the moral order, and the sign of their rejection is such an action as the murder of children to feast on. The stronger the belief that the world ought to be a moral order, the greater the need for the idea of the witch. Again, although the African material provides instances of the justified use of mystical power to harm, this is nowhere regarded as one of the major aims of a religious association. To most students of religion it would surely seem a contradiction in terms. And finally, where we have been able to observe the displacement of a primitive religion by another supported by political authority, we do not find that it survives like a maquis, still less that it follows an independent development, making innovations as time goes on, such as the written compact with the Devil as a substitute for the shedding of blood as the sign of allegiance. What happens is a rather subtle interpenetration of two systems. If the rituals of the displaced religion are abandoned, this is largely because the authorities who would have been responsible for performing them are won over to the new one. What are tenaciously preserved are the magical elements that give individuals the promise of success, protection and remedies in distress – hence, above all, the belief in witchcraft. Africans and Melanesians do not usually reject Christianity until they have tried it, and then they do not profane it but produce modified versions that accord better with their hopes and values.

Most disquisitions on the prosecution of witches in Europe are not concerned with the question why individuals should think their personal enemies are witches, but rather with asking why at a given point in time the authorities of church and state should have become so strongly convinced of the necessity of rooting witches out. Their harmful actions, as they are described in the famous fifteenth-century treatises, the *Formicarius* and *Malleus Maleficarum*, are just those that are associated with witches everywhere. The idea that witches operate in bands is also not new nor peculiar to Europe, but it had not been thought significant in the field of what Mary Douglas has called 'witchcraft control' until the Inquisition authorities began to denounce the 'new sect' of witches in league with the Devil and to demand from accused persons not only confessions of attendance at the Sabbath, but also the denunciation of others.

It has been argued that large-scale trials of witches characterise periods of acute conflicts of religious authority. Yet heresies have been put down by fire and sword without accusations of witchcraft being made. Macfarlane's analysis of the trials in Essex disproves the assumption that they were a manifestation of Puritan zeal, and although the first manuals of witch-lore were written by inquisitors, their work was soon taken over by jurists. Some famous witchcraft trials were concerned with political subversion – notably that of the North Berwick witches, who were supposed to have been led by the King's chief rival, the Earl of Bothwell. In most of them, however, there is no accusation of conspiracy against persons in high places, and the kind of detailed study that would show whether there was a bias against particular categories has never been made. When we read, as we do in Baroja's *World of*

The frontispiece of one of the many editions
(this one from Lyons) of the *Malleus Maleficarum*
('Hammer of Witches'), the guide to the
detection of witches first published by
the Inquisitors Institor and Sprenger in 1486.

the Witches, of panics which swept the Basque country from time to time, we do not know if they were set off by some epidemic or large-scale disaster, or merely the kind of general endemic apprehension that led Essex villages to call in Matthew Hopkins. We are much more often told how the rituals of devil-worship were described than what the witches were charged with in the first place. And when we read of accused persons incriminating others we learn nothing at all of the reasons why particular persons should have been named. But, whatever later sociological investigation might bring to light about the motives at work in particular trials, it is a fact that the fifteenth and subsequent centuries saw a remarkable outburst of interest in the nature and activities of witches.

One comment that can be made on this witch-lore is that it illustrates the constancy with which enormities of the same kind have been attributed by adherents of the dominant religion – whatever it may be at any given time – to those who do not subscribe to it. Before this can happen society must have attained a degree of complexity in which competing religions can exist side by side. Where they do, the rejection by one of the deities of the other – and of its authority, which may be more important – is a real-life fact, not a fantasy, and the organisation of the two into rival congregations is a fact too. In this situation we find that certain of the universal fantasy attributes of the witch are attached to the adherents of the minority religion, notably the ritual murder of children, both for cannibal feasts and to use parts of their bodies for sorcery. This was the accusation made against the Christians when they were a heretical sect of Jews; it was then made against Jews by Christians, and it seems merely perverse in Margaret Murray to suppose that the witches' secret meetings were not deliberately called by the name of a rite of the abhorred religion.

It is because this tendency is by no means dead in the twentieth century that it has seemed worth calling attention to it. It is only

MALLEVS

MALEFICARVM,

MALEFICAS ET EARVM
haeresim frameâ conterens,

EX VARIIS AVCTORIBVS COMPILATVS,
& in quatuor Tomos iustè distributus,

*QVORVM DVO PRIORES VANAS DÆMONVM
versutias, præstigiosas eorum delusiones, superstitiosas Strigimagarum
cæremonias, horrendos etiam cum illis congressus ; exactam denique
tam pestiferâ sectâ disquisitionem, & punitionem complectuntur.
Tertius praxim Exorcistarum ad Dæmonum, & Strigimagarum male-
ficia de Christi fidelibus pellenda ; Quartus verò Artem Doctrinalem,
Benedictionalem, & Exorcismalem continet.*

TOMVS PRIMVS.
Indices Auctorum, capitum, rerúmque non desunt,

Editio novissima, infinitis penè mendis expurgata ; cuique accessit Fuga
Dæmonum & Complementum artis exorcisticæ.

*Vir siue mulier, in quibus Pythonicus, vel diuinationis fuerit spiritus, morte moriatur ;
Leuitici cap. 10.*

LVGDVNI,
Sumptibus CLAVDII BOVRGEAT, sub signo Mercurij Galli.

M. DC. LXIX.
CVM PRIVILEGIO REGIS.

too probable that there are still people in eastern Europe who believe that Jewish ritual is focused on the murder of children, but more interesting examples are to be found in the ascription of witchcraft or obscenity, or both, by dominant sections of a society to disapproved sects or movements.

Voodoo

One such is that known throughout Europe as Voodoo.[4] Nine out of ten laymen, asked for their first association with witchcraft, produce this word; whether they even know what part of the world it comes from is another matter. They suppose it to be a particularly sinister form of witchcraft – as if one were any more sinister, even in imagination, than another – and they would assuredly be disappointed if it was not mentioned in this book.

But it is not witchcraft at all. Lea, great scholar as he was in his own field, supposed the word (associated with French-speaking Haiti) to be derived from 'Vaudois', which in France became a generic term for witchcraft because it was ascribed to the Waldensian heretics. But it is not French at all; it is West African, and is a corruption of the Yoruba word for 'god'. Here, in fact, we do find witchcraft ascribed to the practitioners of a pre-Christian religion by persons hostile to it. Voodoo is the religion that was brought to Haiti by slaves from Dahomey. It has incorporated elements of Christian ritual – definitely not with the intention of blasphemy – as well as of other European ceremonials such as military parades. It is still the religion of the majority of Haitians, although the priests have done their best to suppress it, in some regions with success. The sinister associations that the word Voodoo has acquired date from the centuries when everyone believed in witchcraft, but they have lingered on because, now that those of us who claim to be enlightened no longer suspect our neighbours of bewitching us, we look for the stereotype of evil among peoples who can be regarded as uncivilised. In the early days of Haiti the slave owners feared the sorcery of their slaves, and regarded Voodoo worship, of which they knew almost nothing, as the ritual of a secret society bound together by terrible oaths. They punished persons accused of its practice by torture and branding. The Voodoo worshippers have indeed been described in an official history of Haiti as 'a sort of "black carbonaro" dedicated to the destruction of the Whites', and it would not be surprising if they gave encouragement to the slave rebellion through which Haiti attained independence; the attainment of victory in war is one of the aims of ritual in many religions.

But it was a nineteenth-century British consul, Spencer St John, who in 1884 produced a book making allegations that by now should surprise no reader: namely that Voodoo rites consisted in the murder and eating of children in honour of a serpent god. This was a best seller and was improved on in a second edition, and it was followed up in the twentieth century by the work of a sensational journalist, W. H. Seabrook, who later transferred his talents to West Africa, and an American police chief who was in the island in the period of United States occupation from 1915–33. It would not be too much to say that the sinister reputation this publicity has given to Haiti has been one of its tourist attractions.

But Voodoo is in fact simply a folk religion. Voodoo worshippers are indignant if it is suggested that they are not Catholics. Their pantheon includes Christian saints and African gods. They celebrate both Christmas and a first-fruits ceremony of African type. Their ritual owes little to the Catholic liturgy apart from the use of certain phrases. It consists largely in dancing and singing, and in the course of this individual worshippers are believed to be possessed by spirits, who cause them to act in the manner characteristic of the personality ascribed to the spirit. There are also animal sacrifices. While orthodox Catholics readily see this as a profanation of their religion, it is certainly not intended to be so.

Voodoo priests, who are both men and women, are called to their office by spirits who send them dreams and sickness, and a large part of their activity consists in giving protection against sorcery and in curing its supposed victims. Like African diviners and witch-finders, they are sometimes suspected of 'working with both hands' – that is of using their secret knowledge to harm as well as to cure, particularly to discredit their rivals by impeding the recovery of their patients.

Voodoo worshippers, then, so far from being a secret company of witches or sorcerers, believe that their religion is a defence against just such beings. They believe, as the Ndembu do, that successful men have familiars to work for them. Voodoo belief includes the special feature, part of the Dahomean tradition, that these familiars are dead men brought back from the grave, called zombies.

This complex of beliefs and rituals is what colour prejudice has represented as an unusually dreadful kind of witchcraft.

To conclude this study I will add an example that may seem at first sight to be out of place in a book on witchcraft, since here no question arises of a belief in actions that people with some knowledge of physical causation know to be impossible. The name 'witch-hunt' has been given to many investigations in which there was no question of diabolism or of mystical powers; it is a cliché in discussions of the treatment of political subversion, particularly when this takes the extreme form of attempting to purge whole nations of potential traitors. Such operations rely, like those of Europe's witch-hunters, on 'strong presumptions' rather than evidence, and sometimes on denunciations by former associates which may be thought to have their parallel in the naming by those accused of witchcraft of other members of their coven. Some anthropologists see a parallel in the African idea of the witch as the traitor, the secret enemy of those whose friend he should be and pretends to be; and the strong feeling in African societies against harbouring secret grudges and plotting (it is supposed) revenge certainly has its counterpart on a larger scale in the general fear of unknown persons planning to destroy a whole nation. In so far as the European witch-hunts were directed against persons who were conceived as a 'sect', they can be seen as a precedent for some of the recent campaigns against Communists and spies, both categories of person who would not deny being members of organised bodies.

Mau Mau

Victims of such campaigns have often been falsely accused, but the accusations have been restricted to their political activities. The conspicuous case in which a whole mythology of obscene behaviour has been grafted on a subversive political movement is that of the Mau Mau in Kenya, which has been described, in contrast with other African nationalist organisations, as inherently evil, a form of madness, a 'secret sect . . . aiming at regression towards savagery and witchcraft'.[5] Authoritative writers who have been in general sympathetic to independence movements, and to the specific grievances of the Kikuyu, have singled it out for condemnation. Within Kenya, where there was little such sympathy, particularly after the settler community began to fear for their lives, the explanation of regression to savagery was generally accepted.

Mau Mau differs both from the imaginary witchcraft of European history and from contemporary Communism in that its members did commit murders and did sometimes mutilate the bodies of their victims. But this fact has been made the starting-point of a fantasy picture of obscene rituals, the most interesting feature of which is that it does not correspond to the universal stereotype of the witch. The people who built up this story probably had nothing more specific in mind than the generalised notion of 'savagery' as an inherent quality of colonised peoples. As with the witch-hunters and the Africans themselves, savagery meant the reverse of civilisation, consisting essentially in brutality and obscenity.

The latter was ascribed particularly to the rituals at which men took the oath of loyalty to the cause, and it seems to have been assumed that actions which were disgusting in European eyes somehow stimulated blood-lust. It was believed that the sinister psychological effects of the Mau Mau oath could not be undone unless the tainted person confessed to all his obscenities. Those who refused – perhaps because they had nothing to confess – were described as 'the hard core'. No less an authority than Margery Perham actually wrote of 'breaking the spell'. [6] This was the required preliminary to the rehabilitation of the men who surrendered to the Kenya authorities, and since rehabilitation, whatever it did or did not do to the spirit, was a compulsory stage in the return to freedom and normal life, confessions were made. In addition, information was collected by African members of the security police who were introduced into detention camps.

What is striking is how luridly this information improves on standard ideas about witchcraft. That part of it which has been freely confessed by former members of Mau Mau does describe the performance of pagan rituals, and this in itself is evidence of 'savagery' to the average 'civilised' man, just as it is in Haiti. But the elaborations of cannibalism and of alleged sexual rites during the oath-taking ceremonies are more ingenious than anything to be found in European handbooks of witchcraft or in African mythology. And although there were no such extensive handbooks to guide the hearers of confessions as were so generously provided for the campaigns against witches in Europe, one cannot help feeling that people knew what they were expected to confess.

It is certainly true that the Mau Mau oath-taking ceremonies were modelled on traditional ritual. As in the case of Voodoo, they included elements such as animal sacrifice and the use of blood, but many of those who took the oaths did not regard them as implying the rejection of Christianity; again a parallel with Voodoo. Interestingly enough, although the oath does not mention sorcery, it was understood that persons bound by it would refrain from sorcery against each other. As with every oath which is taken seriously, a breach was supposed to be visited with death. Former adherents of Mau Mau say two oaths were taken, the first undertaking to support the movement, particularly by contributions of money, and the second promising to commit arson or murder when called upon and including the phrase 'even if the enemy be my father or mother, my brother or sister' – a vow that is just what one might expect to find in a secret revolutionary movement, but has been taken in Kenya to imply that Mau Mau adherents actually expected to murder their own close kin.

Bands of men swore oaths before setting out on marauding expeditions, and this inspired some of them with the feeling of loyalty to one another and commitment to a cause that one of them has described.[7] The European version of what happened is given in an anonymous document that was circulated in Kenya during the emergency period.[8] It refers to seventy traditional Kikuyu oaths, and asserts that the 'originators' of Mau Mau put together the 'more powerful features' of them all – a remarkable concession to the belief in magic. By 'powerful features' is apparently meant various sexual obscenities such as the closest observers of African ritual, charged as it is with sexual symbolism, have never come across. The author of this document argues, not very logically, that these obscenities were necessary to inspire those who took the oaths with sufficient blood-lust to bring themselves to pronounce the terrible words. Another interpretation of the rituals is that the obscenities stimulated the necessary blood-lust for the murders and mutilations that were launched by the oath-taking. There is in fact little correspondence between the words of the oaths and the list of atrocities given in the same document.

What inquisitors and lawyers did for Europe, journalists are doing for Africa. Any political movement that resorts to terrorism is now likely to be credited with the alleged characteristics of Mau Mau, as has been for example the Poqo movement in South Africa.

So perhaps the world of modern technology is too complacent in its attitude towards the belief in witches. With the advance of knowledge has come an understanding of physical causes that are unknown in the countries where the belief is still an indispensable element of the cosmology. Few members of technologically developed societies now see events that affect them directly as expressing the plans of a personified deity, even fewer envisage the existence of a personified evil spirit, and none suppose that such a spirit makes human beings his tools. It is easy to look down on societies, contemporary or historical, in which remedies or revenge for disasters are sought in terms of this kind of world-view. But in reality we do not stoically accept that a misfortune either has a rational cause or is inexplicable – that we either know what to do about it or must endure it – and we are no more willing than primitive folk to recognise our own responsibility for our failures. When these are private failures, we are no longer allowed to seek out the person responsible and make him suffer; we have to be content with grumbling about anonymous jealousies or prejudices. This can fairly be regarded as a social advance. But in situations of public anxiety we seem to be little more enlightened. We have the same apprehension of the presence of treachery, and one might even say with Macfarlane that we fear the treachery of those towards whom we have a bad conscience, as the African no doubt does when he asks himself who may have wished to harm him. And we ascribe to the traitor, only in slightly altered terms, those denials of the basic principles of social order that our less well instructed contemporaries ascribe to the witch.

Notes

1 Why should there be witches?

1 R. F. Fortune, *Sorcerers of Dobu*, London, New York, 2nd edn. 1963.
2 R. F. Fortune, *Manus Religion*, American Philosophical Society Memoirs, Philadelphia, 1955.
3 For examples see P. Lawrence and M. J. Meggitt (eds), *Gods, Ghosts and Men in Melanesia*, Melbourne, London, New York, 1965.
4 *see* J. F. M. Middleton, *Lugbara Religion*, London, New York, 1960.
5 E. E. Evans-Pritchard, *Witchcraft, Oracles and Magic among the Azande*, Oxford, 2nd edn., 1950.
6 Ibid., pp. 63–4.
7 M. Wilson, *Good Company*, London, New York, 1951, Chapter 5.

2 What are witches like?

1 M. Wilson, 'Witch beliefs and Social Structure', *American Journal of Sociology*, 1951, pp. 307–13.
2 S. F. Nadel, 'Witchcraft in Four African Societies', *American Anthropologist*, 1952, pp. 18–29.
3 P. J. Morton-Williams, 'The Atinga Cult among the south-western Yoruba', *Bulletin de l'Institut Français de l'Afrique Noire*, 1956, pp. 315–34.
4 J. F. M. Middleton, 'Witchcraft and Sorcery in Lugbara', in J. F. M. Middleton and E. H. Winter (eds), *Witchcraft and Sorcery in East Africa*, London, New York, 1963.
5 R. G. Lienhardt, 'Some notions of witchcraft among the Dinka', *Africa*, 1951, pp. 303–18.
6 Jean Buxton, 'Mandari Witchcraft', in Middleton and Winter, op. cit.
7 T. O. Beidelman, 'Witchcraft in Ukaguru', in Middleton and Winter, op. cit.
8 J. H. M. Beattie, 'Sorcery in Bunyoro', in Middleton and Winter, op. cit.
9 E. H. Winter, 'The Enemy Within', in Middleton and Winter, op. cit.
10 K. M. Burridge, 'Tangu, Northern Madang District', in Lawrence and Meggitt, op. cit.

11 M. Fortes, *The Web of Kinship among the Tallensi*, London, New York, 1957, p. 32.
12 Op. cit., p. 25.

3 Protection against witches

1 B. Reynolds, *Magic, Divination and Witchcraft among the Barotse of Northern Rhodesia*, London, Berkeley, 1963, p. 82.
2 M. J. Field, *Search for Security*, London, Evanston, 1960.
3 M. Wilson, *Communal Rituals of the Nyakyusa*, London, New York, 1959, p. 59.
4 Ibid., p. 61.
5 *The Tiv of Central Nigeria*, Ethnographic Survey of Africa, International African Institute, London, 1953, pp. 81–4.
6 Quoted by J. H. M. Beattie, 'Rituals of Nyoro Kingship', *Africa*, 1959, p. 140.
7 M. Wilson, *Communal Rituals*, pp. 110–1.
8 Anne Sharman, unpublished MS.
9 S. F. Nadel, *Nupe Religion*, London, Chicago, 1954, pp. 190–201.
10 R. S. Rattray, *Religion and Art in Ashanti*, Oxford, 1927, p. 31.
11 P. H. Gulliver, personal communication.
12 B. de Zoete, *Dance and Drama in Bali*, London, New York, pp. 116–33.
13 M. Covarrubias, *Island of Bali*, London, New York, 1937, Chapter 10.
14 Evans-Pritchard, op. cit., p. 178.

4 The detection of witches

1 Hastings ed., *Encyclopaedia of Religion and Ethics*, Edinburgh, 1911, 'Divination'.
2 R. S. Rattray, *Religion and Art in Ashanti*, p. 29, n.l.
3 Mary Kingsley, *West African Studies*, London, 1899, p. 211.
4 A. T. Bryant, *Zulu Medicine and Medicine-Men*, Cape Town, 1966, p. 11.
5 E. E. Evans-Pritchard, op. cit., pp. 175–6.

6 Ibid., p. 253.

7 J. H. M. Beattie, 'Group Aspects of the Nyoro Spirit Medium Cult', *Human Problems in British Central Africa*, 1961, pp. 11–39.

8 I. Schapera, unpublished MS.

9 J. F. M. Middleton, *Lugbara Religion*, London, 1960, pp. 80ff.

10 George Bond, personal communication to the author.

11 J. H. M. Beattie, 'Divination in Bunyoro, Uganda', *Sociologus*, 1964, pp. 44–61.

12 V. W. Turner, *Ndembu Divination: its Symbolism and Techniques*, Rhodes-Livingstone Paper No. 31, Manchester, 1961.

13 M. (Hunter) Wilson, *Reaction to Conquest*, London, New York, 1936, pp. 335–41.

14 M. Griaule, 'Notes sur la divination par le chacal', *Bulletin du Comité d'Etudes Historiques et Scientifiques de l'Afrique Occidentale Française*, 1937. D. Paulme, 'La divination par les chacals chez les Dogon du Sanga', *Journal de la Société des Africanistes*, 1937. H. Labouret, *Les populations dites Bamiléké*, 1935.

15 J. R. Crawford, *Witchcraft and Sorcery in Rhodesia*, London, New York, 1967, pp. 193–4.

16 *Witchcraft among the Azande*, pp. 179–80.

5 Suspicion and accusation

1 R. G. Lienhardt, op. cit., p. 310.

2 R. G. Lienhardt, *Divinity and Experience*, London, 1961, pp. 226–33.

3 M. Wilson, *Good Company*, Chapter 5.

4 M. Wilson, *Communal Rituals*, Chapter 9.

5 M. Wilson, *Rituals of Kinship among the Nyakyusa*, London, New York, 1957, pp. 258–65.

6 M. G. Marwick, *Sorcery in its Social Setting*, Manchester, New York, 1965, chapter 10.

7 The treatment of witches

1 M. Kingsley, *West African Studies*, p. 210.
2 J. H. M. Beattie, 'Sorcery in Bunyoro', in Middleton and Winter, op. cit., p. 46.
3 V. W. Turner, *Ndembu Divination*, p. 11.
4 E. E. Evans-Pritchard, op. cit., p. 26.
5 M. Wilson, *Good Company*, p. 118.
6 J. Buxton, 'Mandari Witchcraft', in Middleton and Winter, op. cit., p. 111.
7 C. Kluckhohn, *Navaho Witchcraft*, Cambridge, Mass., 1944, p. 28.
8 M. Douglas, 'Techniques of Sorcery Control', in Middleton and Winter, pp. 133–42.
9 B. Reynolds, *Magic, Divination and Witchcraft*, p. 122.
10 T. O. Beidelman, 'Witchcraft in Ukaguru', in Middleton and Winter, op. cit., p. 71.
11 D. Paulme, *Une Société de la Côte d'Ivoire: Les Bété*, Paris, 1962, pp. 170–3.
12 George Bond, personal communication to the author.
13 J. La Fontaine, 'Witchcraft in Bugishu', in Middleton and Winter, op. cit., p. 191.
14 E. H. Winter, *Bwamba*, Cambridge, 1956, pp. 117–8.
15 G. Wagner, *The Bantu Kavirondo*, London, New York, 1949, p. 78.
16 M. Wilson, *Communal Rituals of the Nyakyusa*, p. 164.
17 M. Wilson, *Good Company*, pp. 109–19.
18 J. R. Crawford, *Witchcraft and Sorcery in Rhodesia*, London, 1967, p. 65.
19 Ibid., p. 161.
20 S. F. Nadel, 'Witchcraft in Four African Societies', *American Anthropologist*, 1952, p. 29.

8 New ways to deal with witches

1 M. Fortes, 'The Ashanti Social Survey', *Human Problems in British Central Africa*, 1948, p. 6.
2 D. Paulme, op. cit., p. 162.

3 J. C. Mitchell, 'The Meaning in Misfortune for Urban Africans', in M. Fortes and G. Dieterlen (eds), *African Systems of Thought*, London, New York, 1965, pp. 199–201.

4 J. R. Crawford, *Witchcraft and Sorcery in Rhodesia*, pp. 170–1.

5 D. Paulme, op, cit., pp. 186–92.

6 J. R. Goody, *Anomie* in Ashanti? *Africa*, 1957, pp. 356–63.

7 M. J. Field, *Akim-Kotoko*, Accra, 1948, pp. 175–9.

8 M. J. Field, *Search for Security*, pp. 61–76, 98–100.

9 D. Paulme, op. cit., p. 176.

10 J. R. Crawford, op. cit., pp. 45–59, 229.

11 P. Lienhardt, *The Medicine Man*, Oxford, 1967, pp. 190–202.

12 A. I. Richards, 'A Modern Movement of Witch-finders', *Africa*, 1935, pp. 448–61.

13 M. G. Marwick, 'Another Modern Anti-Witchcraft Movement in East Central Africa', *Africa*, 1950, pp. 100–12.

14 George Bond, personal communication to the author.

15 P. Morton-Williams, 'The Atinga Cult among the south-western Yoruba; a sociological analysis of a witch-finding movement', *Bulletin de l'Institut Française de l'Afrique Noire*, 1956, pp. 315–34.

16 B. G. M. Sundkler, *Bantu Prophets in South Africa*, London, New York, 2nd edn., 1961, pp. 109, 238–40.

17 M. W. Murphree, *Christianity and the Shona*, London, 1968.

18 J. R. Crawford, op cit., pp. 227, 229.

9 Fantasy and reality in witch trials

1 R. Bureau, 'Sorcellerie et prophétisme en Afrique noire', *Etudes*, April 1967, pp. 467–81.

2 A. I. Richards, 'The Story of Bwembu', in M. Perham (ed), *Ten Africans*, London, Evanston, 2nd edn., 1963, p. 30.

3 Quoted by W. Notestein, *A History of Witchcraft in England*, London, New York, 1911, p. 71.

4 A. D. Macfarlane, *Witchcraft prosecutions in Essex 1560–1680*, unpublished Ph. D. thesis, 1967.

10 Theories of witchcraft

1 C. Kluckhohn, op. cit., pp. 45–72.
2 M. G. Marwick, 'The Social Context of Cewa Witch Beliefs', *Africa*, 1952, pp. 225–7.
3 M. Wilson, *Rituals of Kinship*, p. 3.
4 M. Kingsley, *West African Studies*, pp. 157–8.
5 S. F. Nadel, 'Witchcraft in Four African Societies', *American Anthropologist*, 1952, p. 23.
6 R. G. Lienhardt, 'Some notions of Witchcraft among the Dinka', *Africa* 1951, pp. 315–6.
7 M. Gluckman, *Politics, Law and Ritual in Tribal Societies*, Oxford, 1965, pp, 223–4.
8 M. G. Marwick, op. cit., pp. 232–3.
9 M. Douglas, 'Techniques of Sorcery Control', in Middleton and Winter. *Witchcraft and Sorcery in East Africa*, pp. 123–41 and 'Witch Beliefs in Central Africa', *Africa*, 1967, pp. 72–80.
10 M. G. Marwick, *Sorcery in its Social Setting*, Manchester, New York, 1965, pp. 14–7.
11 M. Gluckman, op. cit., p. 59.

11 Witchcraft in the Christian context

1 H. C. Lea, op. cit., pp. 537–8, 549.
2 J. Caro Baroja, *The World of the Witches*, London, Chicago, 1964, p. 119.
3 M. A. Murray, *The Witch Cult in Western Europe*, Oxford, 1921.
4 see A. Métraux, *Voodoo*, London, Toronto, 1959.
5 Anonymous, *The Kikuyu Tribe and Mau Mau*, Voice of Kenya, n.d.
6 M. Perham, Introduction to J. M. Kariuki, '*Mau Mau*' *Detainee*, London, Nairobi, 1963, p. xiv.
7 J. M. Kariuki, op. cit. pp. 25–31.
8 Anonymous, 'Mau Mau Oath Ceremonies', mimeographed, n.d.

Bibliography

Anonymous, n.d. *The Kikuyu Tribe and Mau Mau*, Nairobi.

Anonymous, n.d. 'Mau Mau Oath Ceremonies', mimeographed.

Beattie, J. H. M., 1959. 'Rituals of Nyoro Kingship', *Africa*, Vol. 29.

Beattie, J. H. M., 1961. 'Group Aspects of the Nyoro Spirit Medium Cult', *Human Problems in British Central Africa*, No. 30.

Beattie, J. H. M., 1963. 'Sorcery in Bunyoro', in Middleton, J. F. M. and Winter, E. H., eds., *Witchcraft and Sorcery in East Africa*, London, New York.

Beattie, J. H. M., 1964. 'Divination in Bunyoro, Uganda', *Sociologus*, n.s. Vol. 14.

Bohannan, P. J., and L., 1953. *The Tiv of Central Nigeria*, Ethnographic Survey of Africa, London.

Beidelman, T. O., 1963. 'Witchcraft in Ukaguru', in Middleton, J. F. M. and Winter, E. H., eds., *Witchcraft and Sorcery in East Africa*, London, New York, Paris.

Bouquet, A., and Kerharo, J., 1950. *Sorciers, Féticheurs et Guérisseurs.*

Bryant, A. T., 1966. *Zulu Medicine and Medicine-Men*, Cape Town.

Bureau, R., 1967. 'Sorcellerie et prophétisme en Afrique noire'. *Etudes*, Vol. 101.

Burridge, K. M., 1965. 'Tangu, Northern Madang District', in Lawrence P., and Meggitt, M. J., eds., *Gods, Ghosts and Men in Melanesia*, Melbourne, London, New York.

Buxton, J., 1963. 'Mandari Witchcraft', in Middleton, J. F. M., and Winter, E. H. eds., *Witchcraft and Sorcery in East Africa*, London, New York.

Caro Baroja, J., 1964. *The World of the Witches*, London, Chicago.

Crawford, J. R., 1967. *Witchcraft and Sorcery in Rhodesia*, London, New York.

Covarrubias, M., 1937. *Island of Bali*, London, New York.

Cremer, J., 1927. *Les Bobo: Mentalité Mystique*, Paris.

de Zoete, B., 1938. *Dance and Drama in Bali*, London, New York.

Douglas, M., 1963. 'Techniques of Sorcery Control', in Middleton, J. F. M., and Winter, E. H., eds., *Witchcraft and Sorcery in East Africa*, London, New York.

Douglas, M., 1967. 'Witch Beliefs in Central Africa', *Africa*, Vol. 37.

Evans-Pritchard, E. E., 1950. *Witchcraft, Oracles and Magic among the Azande*, Oxford.

Field, M. J., 1948. *Akim-Kotoko*, Accra.

Field, M. J., 1960. *Search for Security*, London, Evanston.

Fortes, M., 1948. 'The Ashanti Social Survey', *Human Problems in British Central Africa*, No. 6.

Fortes, M., 1957. *The Web of Kinship among the Tallensi*, London, New York.

Fortune, R. F., 1963. *Sorcerers of Dobu*, London, New York.

Fortune, R. F., 1935. *Manus Religion*, Philadelphia.

Gluckman, M., 1965. *Politics, Law and Ritual in Tribal Societies*, Oxford.

Goody, J. R., 1957. '*Anomie* in Ashanti?', *Africa*, Vol. 27.

Griaule, M., 1937. 'Notes sur la divination par le chacal'. *Bulletin du Comité d'Etudes Historiques et Scientifiques de l'Afrique Occidentale Française*.

Kariuki, J. M., 1963. '*Mau Mau*' *Detainee*, London, Nairobi.

Kerharo, J., and Bouquet, A., 1950. *Sorciers, Féticheurs et Guérisseurs*, Paris.

Kingsley, M., 1899. *West African Studies*, London.

Kluckhohn, C., 1944. *Navaho Witchcraft*, Cambridge (Mass.)

Labouret, J., 1935. *Les populations dites Bamiléké*, Paris.

La Fontaine, J., 1963. 'Witchcraft in Bugishu', in Middleton, J. F. M., and Winter, E. H., eds., *Witchcraft and Sorcery in East Africa*, London, New York.

Lawrence, P., and Meggitt, M. J., eds., *Gods, Ghosts and Men in Melanesia*, London, Melbourne, New York.

Lea, H. C., 1906. *A History of the Inquisition of the Middle Ages*, London.

Lienhardt, P., 1967. *The Medicine Man*, Oxford.

Lienhardt, R. G., 1951. 'Some notions of witchcraft among the Dinka', *Africa*, Vol. 21.

Lienhardt, R. G., 1961. *Divinity and Experience*, Oxford.

Macfarlane, A. D., 1967. *Witchcraft prosecutions in Essex, 1560–1680*, unpublished Ph. D. thesis.

Marwick, M. G., 1950. 'Another Modern Anti-Witchcraft Movement in East Central Africa', *Africa*, Vol. 20.

Marwick, M. G., 1952. 'The Social Context of Cewa Witch Beliefs', *Africa*, Vol. 22.

Marwick, M. G., 1965. *Sorcery in its Social Setting*, Manchester, New York.

Métraux, A., 1959. *Voodoo*, London, Toronto.

Middleton, J. F. M., 1960. *Lugbara Religion*, London, New York.

Middleton, J. F. M., 1963. 'Witchcraft and Sorcery in Lugbara', in Middleton and Winter, eds., *Witchcraft and Sorcery in East Africa*, London, New York.

Mitchell, J. C., 1965. 'The Meaning in Misfortune for Urban Africans', in Fortes, M., and Dieterlen, G., eds., *African Systems of Thought*, London, New York.

Morton-Williams, P. J. 1956. 'The Atinga Cult among the south-western Yoruba', *Bulletin de l'Institut Français de l'Afrique Noire*, Vol. 18.

Murphree, M. W., 1968. *Christianity and the Shona*, London.

Murray, M. A., 1921. *The Witch Cult in Western Europe*, Oxford.

Nadel, S. F., 1952. 'Witchcraft in Four African Societies', *American Anthropologist*, Vol. 54.

Nadel, S. F., 1954. *Nupe Religion*, London, Chicago.

Notestein, W., 1911. *A History of Witchcraft in England*, New York.

Paulme, D., 1937. 'La divination par le chacal chez les Dogon du Sanga', *Journal de la Societé des Africanistes*.

Paulme, D., 1954. *Les Gens du Riz*, Paris.

Paulme, D., 1962. *Une Sociéte de la Côte d'Ivoire: Les Bété*, Paris.

Perham, M., 1963. Introduction to J. M. Kariuki, *'Mau Mau' Detainee*, London, Nairobi.

Rattray, R. S., 1927. *Religion and Art in Ashanti*, Oxford.

Reynolds, B., 1963. *Magic, Divination and Witchcraft among the Barotse of Northern Rhodesia*, London, Berkeley.

Richards, A. I., 1935. 'A Modern Movement of Witch-finders', *Africa*, Vol. 5.

Richards, A. I., 1963. 'The Story of Bwembu', in Perham, M., ed., *Ten Africans*, London, Evanston.

Sundkler, B. G. M., 1961. *Bantu Prophets in South Africa*, London, New York.

Tauxier, L., 1924. *La Religion Bambara*, Paris.

Turner, V. W., 1957. *Schism and Continuity in an African Society*, Manchester, New York.

Turner, V. W., 1961. *Ndembu Divination: its symbolism and techniques.* Rhodes-Livingstone Paper, No. 31, Manchester.

Wagner, G., 1949. *The Bantu Kavirondo*, London, New York.

Wilson, M., (Hunter), 1936. *Reaction to Conquest*, London.

Wilson, M., 1951. *Good Company*, London, New York.

Wilson, M., 1951. 'Witch beliefs and Social Structure', *American Journal of Sociology*, Vol. 56.

Wilson, M., 1957. *Rituals of Kinship among the Nyakyusa*, London, New York.

Wilson, M., 1959. *Communal Rituals of the Nyakyusa*, London, New York.

Winter, E. H., 1956. *Bwamba*, Cambridge (England).

Acknowledgments

I am especially grateful to Dr A. D. Macfarlane for allowing me to make use of material in his unpublished doctoral thesis *Witchcraft prosecutions in Essex, 1560–1680*. I also acknowledge with thanks the permission given by the following publishers and authors to quote passages: The Clarendon Press and Professor E. E. Evans-Pritchard from *Witchcraft, Oracles and Magic among the Azande*; The Oxford University Press (for International African Institute) and Professor Monica Wilson from *Good Company*; and Mr J. R. Crawford from *Witchcraft and Sorcery in Rhodesia*; Messrs Routledge and Frederick Praeger from *Witchcraft and Sorcery in East Africa*; The Peabody Museum from *Navaho Witchcraft*; Manchester University Press and Professor V. W. Turner from *Ndembu Divination*.

Acknowledgment is also due to the following for illustrations (the number refers to the page on which the illustration appears): 8 Gothenburg Ethnographical Museum; 17, 20, 50, 54, 55, 59, 62, 87, 97, 154–5, 207, 213 British Museum, London (photographed by Axel Poignant); 23, 34, 92, 107, 109 Professor Monica Wilson; 26, 190, 201 Mansell Collection; 41, 73 Faber and Faber Ltd (pictures from Beryl de Zoete *Dance and Drama in Bali*, 1938); 64, 67, 94, 168 Routledge and Kegan Paul Ltd (pictures from S. F. Nadel *Nupe Religion*, 1954); 74 Koninklijk Instituut voor de Tropen, Amsterdam; 81 Dr John Beattie; 89, 132 (adapted) Professor V. W. Turner; 98–9 after M. Griaule 'Notes sur la divination par le chacal' (in *Bulletin du Comité d'Etudes Hist. et Scient. de l'Afrique Occ. Française*, 1937); 117, 119, 121, 122, 123, 124–5, 129 Professor John Middleton; 162, 165, 218 Mme Denise Paulme; 183 His Grace the Archbishop of Canterbury and the Trustees of Lambeth Palace; 192, 228 The Curators of the Bodleian Library, Oxford; 195, 227 Bibliothèque Nationale; 233 British Museum, London.

The map and diagrams were drawn by Victor Shreeve.

Books published or in preparation

Economics and Social Studies

The World Cities
Peter Hall, *London*

The Economics of Underdeveloped Countries
Jagdish Bhagwati, *MIT*

Development Planning
Jan Tinbergen, *Rotterdam*

Human Communication
J. L. Aranguren, *Madrid*

Education in the Modern World
John Vaizey, *London*

Money
Roger Opie, *Oxford*

Soviet Economics
Michael Kaser, *Oxford*

Decisive Forces in World Economics
J. L. Sampedro, *Madrid*

Key Issues in Criminology
Roger Hood, *Durham*

Population and History
E. A. Wrigley, *Cambridge*

History

The Emergence of Greek Democracy
W. G. Forrest, *Oxford*

Muhammad and the Conquests of Islam
Francesco Gabrieli, *Rome*

The Civilisation of Charlemagne
Jacques Boussard, *Poitiers*

The Crusades
Geo Widengren, *Uppsala*

The Ottoman Empire
Halil Inalcik, *Ankara*

Humanism in the Renaissance
S. Dresden, *Leyden*

The Rise of Toleration
Henry Kamen, *Warwick*

The Scientific Revolution 1500-1700
Hugh Kearney, *Sussex*

The Left in Europe
David Caute, *London*

The Rise of the Working Class
Jürgen Kuczynski, *Berlin*

Chinese Communism
Robert C. North, *Stanford*

The Italian City Republics
Daniel Waley, *London*

The Culture of Japan
Mifune Okumura, *Kyoto*

The History of Persia
Jean Aubin, *Paris*

A Short History of China
G. F. Hudson, *Oxford*

The Arts

The Language of Modern Art
Ulf Linde, *Stockholm*

Twentieth Century Music
H. H. Stuckenschmidt, *Berlin*

Art Nouveau
S. Tschudi Madsen, *Oslo*

Palaeolithic Cave Art
P. J. Ucko and A. Rosenfeld, *London*

Primitive Art
Eike Haberland, *Mainz*

Expressionism
John Willett, *London*

Language and Literature

French Literature
Raymond Picard, *Paris*

**Russian Writers and Society
1825-1904**
Ronald Hingley, *Oxford*

Satire
Matthew Hodgart, *Sussex*

The Romantic Century
Robert Baldick, *Oxford*

Philosophy and Religion

Christian Monasticism
David Knowles, *London*

New Religions
Ernst Benz, *Marburg*

Sects
Bryan Wilson, *Oxford*

Earth Sciences and Astronomy

The Structure of the Universe
E. L. Schatzman, *Paris*

Climate and Weather
H. Flohn, *Bonn*

Anatomy of the Earth
André Cailleux, *Paris*

Zoology and Botany

Mimicry in Plants and Animals
Wolfgang Wickler, *Seewiesen*

Lower Animals
Martin Wells, *Cambridge*

The World of an Insect
Rémy Chauvin, *Strasbourg*

Plant Variation and Evolution
S. M. Walters, *Cambridge*
D. Briggs, *Glasgow*

The Age of the Dinosaurs
Björn Kurtén, *Helsinki*

Psychology and Human Biology

Eye and Brain
R. L. Gregory, *Edinburgh*

The Ear and the Brain
E. C. Carterette, *UCLA*

The Biology of Work
O. G. Edholm, *London*

The Heart
Donald Longmore, *London*

The Psychology of Fear and Stress
J. A. Gray, *Oxford*

The Tasks of Childhood
Philippe Muller, *Neuchâtel*

Doctor and Patient
P. Lain Entralgo, *Madrid*

Chinese Medicine
P. Huard and M. Wong, *Paris*

Physical Science and Mathematics

The Quest for Absolute Zero
K. Mendelssohn, *Oxford*

What is Light?
A. C. S. van Heel and
C. H. F. Velzel, *Eindhoven*

Mathematics Observed
Hans Freudenthal, *Utrecht*

Quanta
J. Andrade e Silva and G. Lochak, *Paris*
Introduction by Louis de Broglie

Applied Science

Words and Waves
A. H. W. Beck, *Cambridge*

The Science of Decision-making
A. Kaufmann, *Paris*

Bionics
Lucien Gérardin, *Paris*

Data Study
J. L. Jolley, *London*